GUIDE TO HEDGE FUNDS

OTHER ECONOMIST BOOKS

Guide to Analysing Companies
Guide to Business Modelling
Guide to Business Planning
Guide to Economic Indicators
Guide to the European Union
Guide to Financial Markets
Guide to Investment Strategy
Guide to Management Ideas
Guide to Organisation Design
Guide to Project Management
Numbers Guide
Style Guide

Brands and Branding
Business Consulting
Business Miscellany
Business Strategy
China's Stockmarket
Dealing with Financial Risk
Economics
Emerging Markets
The Future of Technology
Headhunters and How to Use Them
Mapping the Markets
Successful Strategy Execution
The City
Wall Street

Essential Director
Essential Economics
Essential Investment
Essential Negotiation

Pocket World in Figures

GUIDE TO HEDGE FUNDS

What they are, what they do, their risks,
their advantages

Philip Coggan

THE ECONOMIST IN ASSOCIATION WITH
PROFILE BOOKS LTD

Published by Profile Books Ltd
3A Exmouth House, Pine Street, London EC1R 0JH
www.profilebooks.com

Copyright © The Economist Newspaper Ltd, 2008
Text copyright © Philip Coggan, 2008

The greatest care has been taken in compiling this book.
However, no responsibility can be accepted by the publishers or compilers
for the accuracy of the information presented.

Where opinion is expressed it is that of the author and does not necessarily coincide
with the editorial views of The Economist Newspaper.

Typeset in EcoType by MacGuru Ltd
info@macguru.org.uk

Printed in Great Britain by
Clays, Bungay, Suffolk

A CIP catalogue record for this book is available
from the British Library

ISBN 978 1 84668 055 7

The paper this book is printed on is certified by the © 1996 Forest Stewardship
Council A.C. (FSC). It is ancient-forest friendly. The printer holds FSC chain of custody
SGS-COC-2061

FSC
Mixed Sources
Product group from well-managed
forests and other controlled sources

Cert no. SGS-COC-2061
www.fsc.org
© 1996 Forest Stewardship Council

To Robin Coggan (1918–88), who taught me that
there was always more to learn

Contents

Acknowledgements

Writing a book on this subject is rather like painting the Forth Road Bridge. As soon as you have finished, you probably need to start again. The industry is growing and changing so rapidly that it is possible to give only a snapshot of its state at the time of writing.

I was greatly helped by many people within and without the industry, most of whom are individually name checked in the book. All quotes are taken from direct conversations with the author, except where identified. One or two sources have asked to be anonymous.

Special thanks are required for those who gave extra help, notably Robb Corrigan, Peter Harrison, Dan Higgins, Narayan Naik and David Smith. I would also like to thank my colleagues John Prideaux and Arun Rao for their comments after reading parts of the manuscript. Thanks also to Stephen Brough of Profile Books for the original idea and to Penny Williams for her assiduous editing.

Finally, the greatest credit must go to Sandie for her constant love and support and her assiduous reading of the chapters. If there are too many parentheses, it is no fault of hers.

Philip Coggan
October 2007

Introduction

how different / & private equity?

In a small room on the banks of the River Thames, on the site of an old dock, Meg Ryan and Jamie Lee Curtis stand in air-conditioned splendour. All day long, they calculate and analyse and send orders to some 17–18 traders sitting outside. No, the American actresses have not taken up a second career. Meg and Jamie are the names of two of the computer servers in the headquarters of AHL, part of Man Group, one of the largest hedge fund groups in the world. AHL runs billions of dollars on the back of what those computers decide to do.

In his 1980s novel, *The Bonfire of the Vanities*, Tom Wolfe said the investment bankers were the "masters of the universe". That description is now out of date, as Wolfe himself admits. Hedge fund managers have assumed the mantle.

Those men (there are relatively few women) who run the funds have the power to bring down currencies, unseat company executives, send markets into meltdown and, in the process, accumulate vast amounts of wealth. A survey by *Alpha* magazine found that the world's top 25 managers earned more than $14 billion between them in 2006, with the top three taking home – or in their case, several homes – more than $1 billion each.[1] Some of the leading managers have become patrons of the art market, helping drive prices of contemporary artists to new highs.

The very best fund managers are so sought after that they can afford to turn investor money away; being on their client list is a badge of honour akin to joining the more exclusive gentlemen's clubs. Indeed, some would say that investors should be suspicious of any manager who is willing to take their money – the equivalent of Groucho Marx's famous saying: "I wouldn't want to belong to any club that would have ME as a member."

Hedge funds are virtually setting up an alternative financial system, replacing banks as lenders to risky companies, acting as providers of liquidity to markets and insurers of last resort for risks such as hurricanes, and replacing pension and mutual funds as the most significant

1

investors in many companies. Some, such as Eddie Lampert, have even bought companies outright, notably the retailing groups Kmart and Sears; when Daimler sold its Chrysler arm in 2007, the buyer was not another auto giant but a hedge fund/private equity group, Cerberus. They are like wasps at a summer picnic, buzzing round any situation where a tasty feast might be available. If an asset price rises or falls sharply, hedge funds are often to blame. And even when they are not responsible, they will be blamed anyway.

The new managers also have a different style. Unlike traditional bankers, they prefer more casual forms of dress – open-necked shirts and chinos are more common than tailored suits. And they run their businesses from different places – Greenwich, Connecticut and Mayfair rather than Manhattan and the City of London.

This book sets out to explain who the hedge fund managers are and what they do. Most people have probably heard of the term "hedge fund" but have little idea of what it means. That is hardly surprising, since there is no simple, three-word explanation; a survey of international financial regulators in 2006 found that no country had adopted a formal, legal definition of the term. But it is a subject that is hugely important, given the influence of hedge funds. Some say they could even bring down the financial system, a fear that was raised again when markets slumped in the summer of 2007.

Although the term hedge fund is often bandied about in the press, there are few individuals or firms that could rank as household names. Public perceptions of the industry are behind the times. In Britain, the best known example of a hedge fund manager is still George Soros, dubbed "the man who broke the Bank of England" for his role in forcing the pound out of Europe's exchange rate system in 1992; in America, the best known fund is probably Long-Term Capital Management (LTCM), the fund backed by Nobel Prize winners that speculated and lost in 1998, prompting the Federal Reserve (the American central bank) to organise a rescue. But LTCM no longer exists and Soros is better known as a philanthropist and political activist than as a fund manager these days.

Most hedge fund managers would rather stay out of the headlines. They do not want the political hassle that comes with bringing down exchange rates, nor do they want the details of their very large salaries bandied around in the press. (Eddie Lampert was kidnapped in 2003, although in "master of the universe" style, he talked his way free.) A survey of fund managers found that almost three-quarters believe their wealth makes them a target for criminals.[2]

Few hedge funds want to make the size of bets that nearly brought down LTCM. They simply want to make money for themselves and their clients, in an atmosphere devoid of the bureaucracy and stuffiness that often rule at the big financial firms. And they have been pretty successful, certainly in attracting clients.

The managers operate in a world that is bedevilled by jargon (which is why there is a glossary at the end of the book). And it is a world that is ever-changing; indeed, one argument of this book is that the divide between hedge funds and traditional investors is steadily disappearing. In ten years' time, hedge funds may not be a separate category of institution at all.

But let us start with the basics. What is a hedge fund? It is a bit like describing a monster; no single characteristic is sufficient but you still know one when you see one. A report from the Securities and Exchange Commission (SEC), America's financial regulator, on the industry says "the term has no precise legal or universally accepted definition". But we can say that hedge funds have some, or all, of the following characteristics:

- They are generally (but not always) private pools of capital; in other words, they are not quoted on any stock exchange. Investors give the managers money and then share in any rise in value of the fund.
- They are not liquid investments. Investors may only be able to sell their holdings every quarter, and will often need to give advance notice of their intention to do so. Restrictions are even tighter at the start of a hedge fund's life when a lock-up period (which can be two years or more) is imposed. This allows the managers to take risks and buy illiquid assets, without being forced to sell their positions at short notice.
- They are lightly regulated and taxed. Often, they will be registered in some offshore centre such as the Cayman Islands. In return for these privileges, regulators normally try to ensure that only very

wealthy people and institutions (such as pension funds) can invest in them.

◪ They have great flexibility in their ability to invest. They can bet on falling prices ("going short" in the jargon) as well as rising ones. This means they aim to make money even when stockmarkets are plunging, an approach that is known as an absolute return focus.

◪ They have the ability to borrow money in order to enhance returns.

◪ The managers are rewarded in terms of performance, often taking one-fifth of all the returns earned by the fund. Together with an annual charge, this means they carry much higher fees than most other types of fund. Their supporters claim these fees are justified by the skills of the managers involved.

The hedge part of their name springs from the term "hedge your bets". It is generally agreed that an ex-journalist, Alfred Winslow Jones, set up the first hedge fund in the late 1940s. He fancied his ability to pick stocks; in other words, to find those shares that were most likely to rise in price and to avoid those he felt might fall. But he did not want to worry about the overall level of the stockmarket, which might be hit by a rise in interest rates or some political news.

So he tried to hedge his portfolio, buying some shares he felt would rise in price and offsetting them by having short positions in those he felt would fall. Provided his stock picks were correct, he would hope to make money regardless of how the market performed. He was also confident enough in his skills to use borrowed money in an attempt to enhance his returns.

Some modern hedge funds, known as market neutral funds, eliminate market risk completely. But most are not quite so pure. They take directional bets of one kind or another, hoping that a class of shares or bonds or oil or some other asset price will rise. Of course, they may get that bet wrong. That is one of a number of risks that hedge fund investors face. The others include the following:

◪ To the extent that hedge funds use borrowed money, their losses, as well as their gains, can be magnified. For example, if a hedge

fund raises £100m, then borrows a further £300m to invest, a 25%
fall in the value of its portfolio could wipe out all its capital. As an
example, several funds ran into problems in 2007, after they bet
on bonds linked to the riskiest parts of the American mortgage
market. One fund run by Bear Stearns, an investment bank,
became completely worthless; the value of another fell to just nine
cents on the dollar.

- Because the funds are lightly regulated, there is a greater chance
  of fraud. This is especially true because hedge funds are not
  transparent; investors do not know exactly what is in their
  portfolios. Hedge funds desire this opacity so that other investors
  do not know what positions they hold, and thus cannot copy
  their strategies or even bet against them. But in some cases, it
  has transpired that hedge fund managers have been able to lie
  about the profits they have made, or the places where they have
  invested.
- The illiquidity of hedge funds means that, even if investors realise
  that the manager has run into trouble, it could be months before
  they get their money back. Even then, arrangements called "gates"
  may restrict the proportion of an investor's holding that can be
  redeemed.
- The higher fees charged by hedge funds could absorb a large
  proportion of an investor's returns. Indeed, they could more than
  offset any skill the manager might possess.
- The combination of high borrowings and lack of transparency
  could lead to hedge funds taking large positions in some markets.
  In some cases, they may find it impossible to get out of those
  positions without taking huge losses. If enough hedge fund
  managers make the same (wrong) bet, the whole financial system
  could be affected.

Hedge funds: Darwin in action

So why do investors choose to back hedge funds at all? Perhaps the main
reason is that they believe they are giving money to the best and the
brightest; the smartest moneymen in the world.

The managers believe that too. They see themselves embroiled in a daily Darwinian struggle with the markets; they have to make money or perish. Andrew Lo of the Massachusetts Institute of Technology says:[3]

> *Hedge funds are the Galapagos Islands of finance. The rate of innovation, evolution, competition, adaptation, births and deaths, the whole range of evolutionary phenomena, occurs at an extraordinarily rapid clip.*

In 2006, for example, 1,518 new hedge funds were launched, but 717 folded; academic studies suggest that almost half of hedge funds fail to last five years.

Hedge funds are generally established by people with a successful record in trading or fund management. They then persuade their existing clients (or employer) to give them enough capital to make a start, topping that figure up with their own money, or that of friends and relations. The first two years are usually crucial. If they are successful, more clients will come their way. If not, they will have to close the fund.

A brilliant reputation is no guarantee of success. Wadhwani Asset Management was set up by Sushil Wadhwani, who had not only worked for Goldman Sachs and one of the best hedge fund groups, Tudor, but also helped set British interest rates via a seat on the monetary policy committee of the Bank of England. But in late 2006, the group closed its global macro fund, named after the great economist John Maynard Keynes, because of poor returns (just 0.3% in 2006).

Think of the hedge fund manager as a batsman in cricket, or a batter in baseball, dependent on his skill. Some will succeed by taking wild swings and hitting the ball into the crowd; others will score slowly through carefully placed singles. But if they miss the ball too often, they will be out. Most funds fail not because they lose all, or even a significant part, of investors' money; they simply do not earn a sufficient return to keep investors interested or achieve a decent performance fee. As the fund shrinks in size, it becomes uneconomic to carry on.

Nevertheless, it can still be argued, from society's point of view, that there is something bizarre about people becoming so rich from shuffling bits of paper, or manipulating numbers on a computer screen. No doubt the world would be a better place if our greatest minds were working on a cure for cancer or a solution to global warming than trying to bet on the next move in the Japanese yen.

But it is clear that many people are attracted by the buzz of testing themselves in the markets. As a manager, your "score" is known every day (at least to you) as your portfolio rises and falls in value. Luck plays a part, but at the end of a year your performance numbers will tell the world whether you have done a good job. There is no need for career reviews, 360-degree feedback or any other kind of modern management assessment.

Managers work hard. Take a typical day of Nathaniel Orr-Depner, who trades in currencies and commodities for Lionhart, a US group. He gets up at 5am, checks the Bloomberg screens for the Asia closes and is in the office at 6am so he can talk to the firm's Asia office in Singapore. He then talks to the firm's traders in their Wimbledon office in south-west London. This is the best moment of the day for trading since all three major centres are open. But trading continues to be fairly busy through the New York morning when Europe is open. He will then go home and eat some dinner, after which he will talk to the Asian traders as their markets open, so he may not finish till 9 or 10 in the evening. The weekends are more his own, at least from around 4.30 on Friday afternoon to 8.30 on Sunday night, when Asia opens again. With a schedule like that, if you don't enjoy your job, you will not last long.

This ceaseless activity has an enormous effect on financial markets. A 2005 study by Greenwich Associates found that hedge funds accounted for 45% of trading in emerging-market bonds, 57% in distressed debt and 58% in credit derivatives. These proportions have probably risen since then.

Diversification

Another reason investors are willing to give money to hedge funds is that they believe they are getting something different. As already explained, they have the ability to make money from falling as well as rising prices. This absolute return means they aim to make a positive return each year. By and large, they have succeeded. The Hedge Fund Research index[4] shows that, between 1990 and 2006, the only negative year for the average hedge fund was 2002 (a terrible year for markets in general) when investors lost 1.5%.

In contrast, traditional fund managers deliver a "relative return", based on some index or benchmark. They consider they have done well if they beat the index by 3 percentage points. But that may mean, if the index falls by 20%, the client still loses 17%.

Modern financial markets are incredibly sophisticated. Investors can take a whole series of views on a wide range of assets. For example, they can bet on whether an individual company will default on its debt, without worrying about whether interest rates are rising or falling. They can bet on whether bonds that will mature in five years' time will perform better than those that will mature in 30 years. They can take a view on whether markets will become more volatile. They can even speculate on the weather.

As new instruments emerge, hedge funds often have the brains and the computer power to take advantage of them. Traditional investors, such as pension funds and insurance companies, can be slow on the uptake. So for a while, the hedge funds may be able to make some easy profits before the rest of the world catches up.

The strongest claim from hedge funds, and one that is open to considerable dispute, is that their returns are "uncorrelated" with traditional assets such as shares and bonds. What this means is that hedge funds do not always move up and down in line with other assets.

Lack of correlation is an attractive characteristic to risk takers in financial markets. Adding uncorrelated assets to portfolios means investors can receive the same return as before, with a lower level of risk, or a higher return, with the same level of risk.

Short orders

Another argument is that the extra tools hedge funds can use (going short, using borrowed shares) give them advantages over traditional managers. To use another sporting analogy, they have a full set of golf clubs, whereas most managers are given only a driver and a putter.

However, the ability to go short is probably the hedge fund characteristic that causes the most controversy. Short-selling is a long-established practice, with its own little rhyme: "He that sells what isn't his'n, must buy it back or go to prison." It has never been popular. Many people see something underhand in betting on a falling price; it is rather like wishing bad luck on a neighbour. Generally, everyone prospers to some degree when the stockmarket rises, either directly (through shares they own outright or in a pension or insurance fund) or indirectly (as rising wealth leads to higher employment). Stockmarket crashes are usually associated with economic problems.

Companies do not like short-sellers. By driving down the price, they are perceived to be undermining the executives, who are partly motivated by share options. Politicians do not like short-sellers, often because they do not understand the role they play in markets. When a market falls sharply, you can usually find one party hack that will grumble about the manipulation of prices; it even happened after the attacks on New York and Washington in September 2001.

In fact, short-selling is a difficult business. It costs money to borrow shares; short-sellers pay the equivalent of interest. In some markets, there are restrictions on when short sales can be made. Other investors can indulge in "short squeezes", trying to drive prices higher so the short-seller has to cut his position. Whereas there is no limit on how far a share price can rise, a short-seller's gains are restricted; the price can only fall to zero. If you buy a share and the price falls, it gradually becomes a smaller and smaller part of your portfolio; if you short a share and it rises, the position becomes larger and larger. Finally, over the long run, short-selling is a bad bet, since share prices generally rise.

Nevertheless, short-sellers play a useful role in markets. Bubbles do occur, for example during the dotcom boom when companies with no profits and little in the way of sales were worth billions of pounds. Prices can develop momentum effects; as they rise, more investors want to get involved, and that pushes prices up even further. This can drive share prices a long way from fair value. It can lead to the misallocation of capital, a fancy way of saying that bad businesses get funded and good ones fail for lack of interest. Short-sellers, by taking aim at overvalued shares, can bring prices back in line.

Gradually, traditional investors are getting the powers to go short as well, or at least to bet on falling prices. Complex instruments called derivatives allow investors to bet on a host of different factors from currencies, through changes in short-term interest rates to the riskiness (volatility) of the market itself. In Europe, a set of regulations known as UCITS III allows fund managers to use hedge fund techniques. Many big asset management companies, such as Gartmore and Goldman Sachs, have hedge fund arms of their own; some of the big hedge fund groups are launching traditional-style funds.

A growing industry

This convergence reflects the extraordinary growth of the hedge fund business. Everyone wants to get in on the act. In 1990, according to Hedge Fund Research, hedge funds managed some $39 billion of assets, tiny in global terms; by the second quarter of 2007, that figure had grown to $1.7 trillion (or $1,700 billion). The number of funds had increased from 610 in 1990 to 9,767 by March 2007. Until the summer of that year, there was little sign of enthusiasm for the sector diminishing; investors gave managers $60 billion in the first three months of 2007, a record inflow.

America is still the global centre of the industry but Europe, led by London, is catching up. A Financial Stability Forum report in May 2007 found that Europe's share of total hedge fund assets had doubled from 12% in 2002 to 24% in 2006, while Asia's proportion had risen from 5% to 8% over the same period.

That is an awful lot of money and it generates an awful lot of fees. One estimate puts total hedge fund fees in 2005 at $65 billion, and they will have grown significantly since then. This explains why hedge fund managers are able to buy up the swankier apartments in Manhattan and commandeer the best restaurant tables in Mayfair.

Nevertheless, the hedge fund sector is still small in terms of the rest of the fund management industry. Peter Harrison of MPC Investors, a group that manages both hedge and traditional funds, reckons there is some $90 trillion of non-hedge fund assets out there. He thinks investors, particularly pension funds, will gradually push more money into the sector.

But might there be a limit to expansion? Hedge fund managers claim they are "smarter than the average bear". Perhaps they can gain advantages from the techniques they use, or by specialising in small parts of the market where assets might be mispriced. However, it seems unlikely that these opportunities are endless. As more money pours into the industry, mispriced assets will be harder and harder to find; in the jargon, they will be arbitraged away.

Average hedge fund returns certainly seem to be falling. In the 1990s, it was common for hedge funds to earn 20% a year; in 2004/05, returns were in the high single digits. According to Dresdner Kleinwort, an investment bank, hedge returns have been trending down since 1990 at a rate of around 1.2 percentage points a year.

Of course, the first decade of the 21st century has been a much more difficult time for asset prices in general than the 1990s were. Returns everywhere have been falling. But lower market returns mean that the fees paid to hedge fund managers take a bigger bite out of the net return to investors.

Hedge fund managers market themselves on the basis of their skill, or alpha as it is known in the jargon. Pure market exposure, in contrast, is known as beta. It is agreed that investors should be willing to pay high charges for alpha since it is a rare property. But beta is a commodity, a seaside postcard relative to alpha's Picasso.

One of the big questions for hedge funds over the coming years is whether there is enough alpha to allow the continued expansion of the industry. Already there are attempts to produce cut-price versions of hedge funds, which offer similar returns at much lower fees. Perhaps one day even smarter, but cheaper, businesses will replace the hedge fund giants.

Investors

Who are the people who give money to hedge funds? For tax and regulatory reasons, few small investors – the people with just a few thousand pounds or dollars in savings – have been able to gain access to the sector. Historically, the rich (high net worth individuals and family trusts) were the main backers of the hedge fund titans.

But this has slowly been changing. A survey by Greenwich Associates in 2007 found that the rich now owned around 21% of hedge fund assets. But institutional investors – charitable endowments and pension funds – owned around 25%. However, another quarter of the industry was owned by funds-of-funds which could be owned by anyone, pension funds and the rich included. So it is hard to say definitively where the balance of power lies.

The development that gets the industry most excited is the growing enthusiasm for hedge funds among pension funds. With many trillions of assets under their management, this is a potentially huge prize. Progress is slow but steady. A survey by Mercer, a consultancy group, in May 2007 found that 6% of British pension funds invested in hedge funds, compared with 9% of those in continental Europe. In America, an April 2006 survey by Greenwich Associates found that nearly a quarter of corporate pension plans invested in the sector. The Bank of New York predicted[5] that institutional demand for hedge funds would grow from $360 billion in 2007 to more than $1 trillion by 2010.

Why are pension funds interested in hedge funds at all? After all, they have traditionally paid low fees for fund management – less than one percentage point with no performance fee in many instances. Backing a hedge fund would appear to be handing over their members' money to multimillionaires.

Indeed, pension fund trustees have traditionally been suspicious of the hedge fund industry. The reason has been partly the fee issue but more generally two other perceptions: the idea that hedge funds are risky and the lack of transparency about the way hedge fund managers generate their returns. The risk issue relates to collapses such as LTCM and a few scandals in America. But the plunge in stockmarkets during 2000–02 brought home to trustees that equities can be risky too, and that hedge funds can hold up well during market crises. And the willingness of consultants to get involved in hedge fund analysis has given trustees some comfort on the transparency front.

Chris Mansi of British actuarial consultants Watson Wyatt says:

> Pension funds have traditionally owned equities and bonds and not much else. Since bonds are a close match for their liabilities, that means the risk budget has been highly focused on the equity risk premium.

The premium to which Mansi is referring is the excess return equities have to offer to compensate investors for the extra risks involved in owning them. However, Mansi says there are other types of risk, including credit risk (in the bond market), illiquidity risk (some investors cannot own illiquid assets, which means that those who can earn excess returns) and skill. Hedge funds represent an exposure to this skill factor.

But a lot depends on whether you can find the right managers. Mansi says:

> It is hard to take the view that the average hedge fund investor is going to be successful going forward. Either there is an unlimited number of talented people or there have to be new sources of return for hedge fund managers to exploit.

Hedge funds are only one of the "alternative assets" that pension funds have been pursuing. Other asset classes include private equity, real estate and commodities. Many funds have been trying to follow the Yale example, after the American university endowment, which has enjoyed remarkably successful returns thanks to a highly diversified portfolio. In Britain, the Wellcome Foundation, a medical charity, has been moving in this direction, and a Dutch pension fund, ABP, has also widened its investment horizons.

Fees

Hedge fund managers charge a lot more than conventional managers, although their fees are similar to those charged in the private equity industry (firms that buy up companies, restructure the businesses and sell them again). The fee structure can vary but the standard model is "2 and 20", that is an annual fee of 2% of the assets under management and a performance fee of 20% of the returns that the portfolio produces (after the annual fee is deducted). So if the portfolio returns 12%, the hedge fund manager would take its 2% annual fee, and then a further 2%, representing one-fifth of the net return.

Successful fund managers can charge more; one of the best-known high earners was Renaissance Technologies, which charged an astonishing 5 plus 44 on its Medallion fund. However, the fund in question no longer looks after money for outsiders, even though they would have been more than happy to pay; until 2006, its annual average return was more than 35%, even after fees.

There are some protections for investors, notably a high water mark system that allows performance fees to be charged only if the previous peak has been reached. Say a fund was launched at $100 and rose to $122 in its first year. A 2 and 20 manager could take 6 percentage points of fees

(2 annual and 4 performance). But if the fund then dropped in value to 110, the 122 mark would have to be passed before performance fees could be charged again.

Even with that safeguard, hedge fund fees mean that managers really do need some skill (or a lot of luck) to deliver decent returns to investors. Furthermore, many hedge funds trade frantically, turning over their portfolios several times in the course of a year. This incurs considerable costs. When you buy and sell a share, there is a spread between the prices a marketmaker will offer you (that is how marketmakers earn the bulk of their profits). Then there are brokers' commissions (hedge funds often get their ideas from stockbrokers), borrowing costs when taking a short position, custody fees (someone has to keep safe hold of the assets in the fund) and so on. According to Dresdner Kleinwort, all these costs add up to 4–5% a year.

If the hedge fund client wants a net return of 10% a year, the hedge fund portfolio may need to generate 18–19% a year before costs and fees. This is a tall order in a world where cash and government bonds pay 4–5%. In a good year, the stockmarket can return 20%, but as already explained hedge funds are not supposed to be offering simple exposure to the stockmarket.

Costs can be even higher for those clients who use a fund-of-funds manager to invest in the sector. It is understandable why so many choose to do so. These intermediaries can sort through the several thousand managers on offer, attempt to understand their complex strategies and, most importantly, check that their backgrounds and systems are above board. In addition, because the best hedge funds are often closed to new investors, getting access to those managers may require the services of a fund-of-funds, which will have an established relationship with the industry's elite. But fund-of-funds managers take an annual fee (normally 1%) plus a performance fee for their trouble.

These high fees are attracting many traditional fund management groups to open hedge funds and encouraging investment banks to buy, or take stakes in, hedge fund managers. The industry is gradually becoming mainstream. But this is still a weird and wonderful world, with lots of different creatures being dubbed hedge funds, even though they have strikingly different characteristics. The taxonomy of that world is the subject of the next chapter.

1 Hedge fund taxonomy

It is hard to make sweeping statements about hedge funds. Some take extravagant gambles; others control risks carefully. Some love to be in the public eye; others would be mortified at a mention in the *Wall Street Journal* or *Financial Times*. Some deal in exotic instruments such as credit derivatives; others simply buy and sell shares like an ordinary fund manager.

That is why commentators have to be careful before pronouncing that hedge funds are buying oil, or that hedge funds have lost a bundle in the Japanese stockmarket. For every hedge fund on one side of the trade, there is likely to be another that is betting in the opposite direction. This is both a source of strength and of weakness for the sector. The strength is that a market fall is highly unlikely to ruin all hedge funds. In August 2007, when everyone was concerned about a financial crisis, the average hedge fund lost just 1.3%, according to Hedge Fund Research. But the weakness is that, if hedge funds are on both sides of the table, their activities sound increasingly like a zero sum game – a game for which investors are paying extremely high fees.

The sheer variety of hedge funds means that investors need to be careful about what they are buying. The freewheeling style of George Soros or Julian Robertson (who ran the Tiger funds) is far less common these days. The institutional clients of the industry (pension funds, university endowments and private banks) like funds that do "what it says on the tin".

The result is that the industry is nowadays divided into a wide variety of sectors. These divisions are far from hard and fast; index providers who categorise the industry rarely have exactly the same descriptions. Some are pretty cynical about the whole exercise. "Hedge fund strategy descriptions are largely there for marketing purposes," says Steven Drobny of Drobny Global Advisors, an expert on the industry.

Part of the difficulty in defining hedge funds is their sheer complexity. Guy Ingram of consultants Albourne Partners says: "It is like cartographics.

You have the problem that you are drawing in only one dimension." Ingram says there are really three: the exposure of the funds (whether they are net long or short); the style of management, whether they use computer models (quants, in the jargon) or human judgment; and the asset class they invest in. Mapped on that basis, it is clear that many strategies sit on the boundary of two or more sectors.

For this book's purposes, we can roughly divide the industry into four categories:

- ◪ The first is the Winslow Jones style of managers, those who play the stockmarket with both long and short positions.
- ◪ The second can be described as arbitrage players, those seeking to exploit inefficient areas of the financial markets such as convertible bonds (see page 20).
- ◪ The third can be dubbed directional, those investors who attempt to exploit trends or inconsistencies in a wide range of markets, using either their own judgment or some kind of computer model.
- ◪ The fourth is funds that are known as event-driven, those that exploit a particular situation, such as a merger or a bankruptcy.

Out of these four broad categories, 10–20 subcategories can be created.[1]

Because there is no universal agreement on sector classification, it is hard to be definitive about how large the individual sectors are. The fund-of-funds group GAM, which keeps its own database, reckons that, at the end of April 2007, there were some 6,454 funds of which around half (3,287) were equity-linked. There were some 1,775 arbitrage funds but of those some 525 funds were in sectors that fall into the event-driven category used in this book. Lastly, there were 1,392 directional or trading funds.

What is clear is that the industry is much more diversified than it used to be. As of 1990, Hedge Fund Research reckoned that 71% of assets were in global macro funds; by mid-2007, the largest sector (equity long-short) had less than 28%, while macro funds were just 11% of the total.

Equity funds

Equity long-short

Perhaps the fastest-growing hedge fund strategy is equity long-short, probably because of its familiarity to both potential managers and clients. For a manager coming from a long-only background, equity long-short seems a natural first step. It takes advantage of his ability to pick stocks. For investors, the style is closest to the traditional active management they are used to, but with the potential appeal of reducing market risk.

But this does not mean it is easy. Managers can find it difficult to make money out of their short positions (for reasons explained in the Introduction). If the manager has a high exposure to the market, he starts to look like a traditional long-only fund, with much higher fees. Furthermore, clients may feel they are paying for beta (market exposure) rather than alpha (skill).

However, if the manager reduces his exposure to the market, he will probably find he is lagging the major indices during bull phases. That may tempt clients to switch away from hedge funds and back towards the long-only category. If hedge fund managers end up chasing the market, they can get caught out by a sudden downturn, especially if they are using leverage; this happened to the earliest generation of managers, many of whom were wiped out by the bear market of the mid-1970s. The SEC found 140 hedge funds operating in 1968, but a Tremont Partners survey in 1984 could discover only 68.

Some managers try to avoid these problems by having a semi-permanent asset allocation, aiming to be, say, a net 80% long most of the time. Others want the flexibility to use their market timing skills (although it is far from clear that stock-pickers will also be astute at guessing the overall direction of the market).

Despite the potential problems, long-short funds keep being created. "There are an awful lot of long-short funds because there are few barriers to entry," says Simon Ruddick of Albourne Partners. One obvious reason the long-short sector is home to so many funds is that, like ice-cream, it comes in many flavours. Long-short funds can be geographical, focusing on the American market, Europe as a whole (or as individual countries) and emerging markets. They can also be sectoral, focusing on individual industries such as biotechnology or energy. The managers can be traditional stock-pickers or quants, using computer models.

The sector also intersects with a fast-growing product known as the 130–30 fund. Such funds (named after their long-short proportions) are often not constructed as hedge funds but are a way for institutions to benefit from hedge fund techniques (see Chapter 6).

Market neutral

This style could be seen as the purest form of hedge fund investing, relying entirely on the manager's skill. Long and short positions are equally matched so that the direction of the market should have no effect on performance (hence the name of the strategy). This approach is usually based on pairs trading, with the manager finding similar stocks and buying the one he likes and shorting the other – an obvious example would be to go long BP and short Shell.

The trouble with this approach, says Dan Higgins of Fauchier Partners, a fund-of-funds group, is that there are no perfect pairs. Managers can delude themselves into thinking they are taking no thematic risk, but when all the positions are added up you find that they are exposed to dollar risk, commodity risk or some other factor.

Furthermore, it can be rare for the manager to have equal convictions about his long and his short positions. So the client finds that while the manager is making money on his long positions, he is losing it on his shorts. Even if a manager is skilful, the difference between the performance of his long and short positions may be small; hence managers use gearing to enhance returns, which introduces another layer of risk.

Nevertheless, those investors who can find skilful market neutral managers can clearly add a useful source of diversification to their portfolios.

Short-selling

This is probably the most difficult of all the sectors for the managers concerned; few have made a long-term success of it. Some of the problems facing short-sellers have already been explained. For a start, they are fighting the tide; markets generally go up over the long term. Second, exchanges can impose restrictions on short-sellers and even when they do not, it can be difficult (and costly) for short-sellers to borrow the stock they need to sell. Third, the mechanics are unfavourable; the maximum gain that can be achieved is 100%, while the loss is potentially infinite and losing positions steadily form a greater and greater part of the portfolio.

Companies can also be aggressive towards short-sellers, mounting press campaigns against them. And because the overall level of short positions in a stock have to be disclosed, other investors can try to push the market against them, forcing the price higher "in a short squeeze", reasoning that, eventually, the shorts will have to crack and buy back the stock.

Nevertheless, some investors like to have short-selling funds within their portfolios as a diversifier for when markets fall. But even in bear markets for shares such as 2000–03, short-sellers have not done quite as well as investors might have expected. As a result, there are few players in this business; David Smith of GAM reckons there are only around 25 short-sellers operating in the world.

Arbitrage funds

Arbitrage funds aim to exploit anomalies in the mispricing of two or more securities. For example, take Dixons, once one of the UK's leading high-street retailers, and Freeserve, once one of the hottest internet stocks. There was a point during the dotcom boom when Dixons' stake in Freeserve was worth almost as much as the market value of Dixons itself. Unless you thought the high-street chain was worthless, it made sense to buy shares in Dixons, short shares in Freeserve and wait for the anomaly to right itself.

It is important to make the distinction between riskless arbitrage and other types. Riskless arbitrage occurs when the same asset is selling for different prices at the same time. Provided that the transaction costs are smaller than the gap in prices, it is possible to profit by buying at the low price and selling at the high. Such chances are rare. Most arbitrage strategies are based on the theory that normal relationships between asset prices should hold. But they might not, which is why risk is involved.

The theoretical attraction of arbitrage funds, according to Higgins, is that they are less correlated with the overall stockmarket. The problem is that with lots of clever people scanning the markets every second, arbitrage opportunities are likely to be fleeting. If enough capital is chasing these opportunities, returns are likely to fall.

"The main driver of the returns is the supply of the inefficiencies relative to the amount of capital invested," says Higgins. Thus the funds generally perform best after a period of great volatility, when there are wider spreads to be arbitraged away. For example, there were some attractive opportunities after the collapse of Enron and WorldCom, two big American companies mired in scandal, in 2002.

Convertible arbitrage

The convertible arbitrage sector has recently provided a textbook example of how too much capital can drive down returns. It invests in convertible bonds: fixed income instruments that give investors the right to switch into shares at a set price.

Such bonds go through spurts of popularity, usually when stockmarkets are rising. In such circumstances, investors like them because they give them a geared play on the stockmarket (the bond becomes much more valuable when the market price of the shares rises above the price at which the shares can be converted). Companies like them because they carry lower interest rates than conventional bonds; it seems as if the market is giving them a subsidy.

But hedge fund managers looked at these bonds in a more sophisticated way, as a bond with a call option attached (a call option is the right to buy an asset at a certain price). They reckoned that these call options were often underpriced, something they could calculate by looking at the price of options on the underlying shares. (In the jargon, the implied volatility of the bond was lower than the implied volatility of a conventional option.) As a result, convertible arbitrage managers would take advantage by buying the bonds and selling short the shares (using a technique known as delta hedging to calculate the number of shares they should short). The potential for profit arose because companies had sold the right to buy shares at too cheap a price. "In effect, it was a transfer of wealth from minority shareholders to the arbitrage community," says Ruddick.

How did managers make money? The simple version is that they would wait for the bond to be repriced relative to the shares. The more complicated version is that either the value of the bond would rise (its implied volatility would go up) or the manager would profit from the hedging process (since delta hedging would naturally lead him to buy low and sell high).

There were further advantages to the strategy. Corporate bonds pay a yield, which the fund would accumulate, offsetting the cost of selling the shares short. Managers also gear up the returns by using borrowed money.

According to Higgins: "In the early years of the strategy, it had very low volatility and high returns." Naturally, the promise of easy money lured a lot of capital into the sector. The bonds steadily became less cheap and then started to trade at a premium to their underlying value. Higgins says:

> By 2001–02, the trade was getting crowded. In 2002, it got bailed out by higher volatility. You were buying expensive fire insurance, but there was a fire.

The crunch eventually came in 2005. A lot of convertible arbitrage funds lost money, and many were closed.

As a result, the cycle started again in 2006. The withdrawal of capital from the sector meant there was less competition for profitable opportunities and the surviving convertible managers started to perform again. Some managers may also have moved into capital structure arbitrage, which looks across all the instruments issued by a company to see if one looks cheaper than another. For example, if a company is in trouble, a manager could buy the senior debt (with the greatest rights over the assets) and short the subordinated debt (which has far fewer rights). If the company then went bust, the manager would make more money on the short position than he would lose on the long. With more and more instruments being created (such as credit derivatives), capital arbitrage may be a rapidly expanding sector.

Statistical arbitrage

Those involved in statistical arbitrage (stat arb, for short) are the real rocket scientists of the industry, using highly sophisticated models to try to find statistical relationships between various securities. This approach can be described as quantitative, and the managers are also known as quants. (The quants are not confined to the statistical arbitrage sector; they can also be found among long-short and market neutral funds and, indeed, in the long-only world.)

A prime example is Jim Simons of Renaissance Capital (see Chapter 2), a firm that focuses on hiring scientists, not fund managers. The idea of statistical arbitrage is that certain securities are linked; for example, some companies have dual classes of shares. Such securities will not always move exactly in line but will move within a range of each other's values, say 90–100%. When the upper or lower bands of that range are reached, a statistical arbitrage fund will bet on reversion to the mean. Unlike managed futures funds (see below), which bet that a trend will continue, stat arb funds bet that it will stop.

Some of these profitable opportunities may last for only a fraction of a second. So, rather like gunslingers in the wild west, stat arb managers have to worry that there will always be someone faster than they are. There has been a kind of arms race to execute trades as quickly as possible, with trades now executed in a thousandth of a second. Some even site their computers as close as possible to the stock exchange to minimise the time it takes their orders to travel down the wires. Stat arb managers also need markets to be liquid. Higgins says:

> There is clear evidence that they need very deep pockets to invest in research and development and to develop computer power.

Because the models are so sophisticated, it is hard for managers to explain how they work (indeed, it is not in their interest to give too much detail away). The investor can only really be guided by their track record – not always a great predictor of future performance – and take their brilliance on trust.

According to Ruddick: "For a 10–15 year period, stat arb was one of the most reliable generators of value." He says the funds were really acting as synthetic marketmakers. They benefited because many investors were trying to offload large positions on the market and there were not enough players with capital to take the other side of those positions; this gave the stat arb funds a chance to make a profit.

One source of profit disappeared when Wall Street shifted from quoting share prices in fractions (sixteenths, eighths) to quoting in decimals. That allowed for much keener prices (lower spreads) and one-third of all marketmaking profits disappeared overnight. Since then, stat arb funds have faced keen competition from the proprietary trading desks of investment banks, from order matching systems, which link buyers and sellers without going through a marketmaker, and from specialist operators.

It is a tough business. Quant managers were hit particularly hard in the market turmoil of July and August 2007, when their models appeared to break down and many (including Renaissance) suffered far greater losses than they had been expecting. The problem was that quant managers had become such a large part of the market that they were all holding similar positions; when they attempted to sell (to reduce their leverage), it was rather like a crowd trying to leave a theatre via a narrow door. The prices of the stocks they owned plunged because of an excess of sellers. Clifford Asness of AQR Capital, one of the leading quant players, described it as a "deleveraging of historic proportions" in a letter to his investors.

Fixed income arbitrage

The fixed income arbitrage sector carries the burden of Long-Term Capital Management (LTCM),[2] the huge (and hugely-geared) hedge fund that collapsed in 1998. LTCM was founded by John Meriwether and a bunch of fixed income traders from Salomon Brothers who tried to replicate their success at the investment bank. Thanks to their record and their contacts, they received a lot of backing, and had powerful people as investors (it helped that two Nobel Prize winning economists advised them).

Their essential idea was that some securities in the market were irrationally priced; for example, the Treasury bond market used to have the 30-year issue as a benchmark. Everyone would want to own that bond, hence a bond with only 29 years till maturity would trade at a discount. If this discount got too wide, it would eventually correct (after all, the bonds were guaranteed by the American government) and those who bought the 29-year bond would make a profit. Because prices got only slightly out of line, it was necessary to use a lot of leverage to make money.

LTCM essentially ran into two problems. The first was what is known as the "gamblers' fallacy". You might have a system for beating the casino; for example, doubling up after every losing bet. This might work, but only if you have infinite capital. If luck runs against you, you will be bankrupt before you succeed. This is what happened to LTCM. When

Russia defaulted in 1998, everyone wanted to own riskless assets. But LTCM's bets were essentially all of one type: to be long of risky assets and short of riskless ones. Spreads widened more than history suggested they would. Eventually, they should have returned to normal (indeed, those who took over LTCM's positions made money). But because of the leverage, LTCM ran out of money before that happened.

The second, and related, problem was that LTCM's models did not allow for the kind of market move that occurred. In part, this was because extreme events occur more often in the financial markets than conventional models assume. This is particularly the case when markets are illiquid and one player (such as LTCM) has a large position.

There is an old story of an enthusiastic investor who piled into a penny stock (a small company with a share price of a few pence or cents). As he bought, he was delighted to see the share price move higher, so he increased his position. Finally, having more than doubled his money, he called his broker and said, "Now I'd like to sell". "Who can you sell to?" asked the broker. "You were the only buyer." LTCM faced the problem that it had large positions that were well known to everyone in the market. It had to offload those positions at a fire sale price.

There is no reason, in theory, why current fixed income arbitrage managers should run into the same problems. They have two main avenues for profit, the yield curve and credit spreads. On the yield curve, as in the LTCM example above, they can bet on its shape. Traditionally, long-term bonds have yielded more than short-term bonds; if the shape does not conform to this pattern, they can bet on a return to the status quo. On credit, they can bet that wide spreads will narrow or that narrow spreads will widen. However, it is easier for them to bet on narrowing than widening because of the way the trade works: narrowing involves buying a higher-yielding bond and shorting a lower-yielder. As a result, the trade has a positive carry (it earns interest income). Betting on wider yields would mean losing money in the short term until the spread corrected.

The sector has been given a lot more flexibility by the development of credit derivatives, particularly credit default swaps (CDSs) and collateralised debt obligations (CDOs). The former allow investors to insure their bonds against default, or alternatively to bet that default will occur; the latter slice and dice portfolios of bonds into different tranches, based on risk. The result is that the corporate debt market is much more liquid. But the potential for risk-taking has increased sharply, as the problems facing hedge funds in the summer of 2007 illustrated.

Directional funds

Global macro managers

Global macro managers dominated the industry in the early 1990s but have since become much less significant. As well as George Soros, the likes of Julian Robertson and Michael Steinhardt were renowned for making big plays on currencies, bonds and stockmarkets. But Steinhardt retired in 1995 and Robertson gave up the ghost in 2000. Each suffered problems towards the end, with Steinhardt making big losses in the bond market sell-off of 1994 and Robertson being caught out by the dotcom boom of the late 1990s.

Soros continues, with more than $11 billion under management as of the end of 2006. But he is better known for his political and philanthropic works these days; there has been no triumph on the scale of his bet on sterling's devaluation in 1992.

A separate group of managers developed from the commodities markets, particularly the likes of Paul Tudor Jones, Bruce Kovner (of Caxton) and Louis Bacon (of Moore Capital). These are generally known as managed futures managers (see next section).

Global macro is hard to define. As Drobny writes in his book *Inside the House of Money:*[3]

> *Global Macro has no mandate, is not easily broken down into numbers or formulas, and style drift is built into the strategy as managers move in and out of various investing disciplines depending on market conditions.*

That makes the style a difficult sell now that the dominant investor class in hedge funds is institutional. The institutions, and the consultants who advise them, like to put hedge funds in a box so they can work out how much of their money is devoted to a particular asset class or risk approach. They like predictability and dislike style drift. In contrast, a global macro manager appears to be saying: "I'm really clever. Trust me to navigate the markets."

These days, there may be a general cynicism among investors about the ability of hedge fund managers to make big successful bets on macro events such as devaluations. With the advent of the euro, there are fewer fixed exchange rates to aim at and those that remain, such as China's, have capital controls and are thus more difficult to speculate against.

Some global macro managers have diversified into becoming multi-strategy funds, a term that sounds more up-to-date but still, in essence, depends on the ability of one man (or small group of men) to allocate capital to asset classes based on his view of the world. The key formal difference between multi-strategy and global macro is that the former allocates money to sub-managers as he sees fit and the latter is running all the money himself. In practice, the divide is not quite so sharp, since a big global macro manager will delegate certain asset classes to different trading teams.

Managed futures or commodity trading advisers

Technically speaking, this is not really a hedge fund sector at all. Its name springs from its regulatory origins; these are funds that deal in the futures markets and, as a consequence, are overseen by the Commodity Futures Trading Commission in Chicago. They are required to disclose their activities, particularly the costs incurred in trading. "It's a much cleaner business than the hedge fund business," says David Harding, one of the pioneers of the sector; he set up AHL and now has his own firm, Winton Capital.

Nevertheless, commodity trading advisers (CTAs) are generally lumped in with the hedge fund industry, perhaps because they often take big risks and can earn outsized returns and perhaps because some of the big names of the hedge fund industry, such as Tudor Jones, started in this sector. But they also attract a lot of suspicion, and some fund-of-fund investors will not include them in their portfolios. Recent performance has also been disappointing with single digit returns in each of 2004, 2005 and 2006, according to Hedge Fund Research. Nevertheless, one estimate says that managed futures funds ran $170 billion of assets at the end of 2006.[4]

One of the leading managers, Anthony Todd of Aspect Capital, says: "Managed futures is the most misunderstood sector." However, this is hardly surprising when managers are so reluctant to explain exactly what they do. Firms are highly dependent on "black box" models – computer programmes that scour the market for profitable opportunities. If a manager gives away how the model works, his business could be destroyed since another manager could copy it. But that limits what they can tell clients. The best they can say is: "We have a system that has beaten the market in the past. Here are the results. Trust us when we say this will also work in the future."

Not everyone is comfortable about this arrangement. David Swensen, who runs the fabulously successful Yale endowment fund (and has been a big investor in hedge funds), has said: "You cannot be a partner with somebody who has a black box."[5]

So what are the systems trying to do? According to Todd:

> *Markets are not completely efficient.*[6] *There is a tendency for trends to persist and there is a tendency for investors to act as a herd. We believe such trends will exist whatever market you look at and over multiple timeframes.*

He says his firm attempts to exploit trends on a systematic basis, covering a wide range of markets (90 or so). The business started in the commodity markets (hence the CTA name) and uses futures contracts, a cheap way of getting exposure to an asset class.

Markets do indeed seem to show trends. They have long periods of rising prices (bull markets) interspersed with falling prices (bear markets). Once a managed futures fund believes such a trend has set in, they will jump on the bandwagon. They are thus vulnerable to two things: a sudden break in the trend (such as a crash), or a period of range-bound markets, where prices keep changing direction. "We don't buy CTAS because we think they get whipsawed when trends change," says Higgins. Like the stat arb funds, CTAS suffered in the market turmoil of summer 2007.

A further problem is that they are not the only ones looking for such trends. If it was obvious that a bull market was under way, lots of people would spot it and prices would rise quickly, before the managed futures fund had positioned itself. As Todd admits, "The difficulty is that markets are always developing. The half-life of any given systematic approach is shrinking." That means managers have to devote a lot of money to research, so they can keep ahead of the game. And it also means they have to be adaptable without changing tactics so often that clients start to wonder whether they are guessing.

The need for new ideas is such that CTAs often have a lot of mathematicians and academics on their staff. Winton has set up two academies, one in Hammersmith in west London and the other in Oxford, and the Man Group (the parent company of AHL) has sponsored the Oxford-Man Institute of Quantitative Finance. It all sounds a long way from *Brideshead Revisited*.

Tim Wong, chief executive of AHL, says his firm spends a lot of time trying to improve on the execution of its ideas. He says:

> It's difficult to find new ideas where you can guarantee alpha,
> but if you lower your trading costs, you know exactly what
> return you are going to get.

Some argue that managed futures funds offer a poor trade-off between risk and reward (in technical terms, a low Sharpe ratio) compared with other hedge funds. This is true. But Todd argues that funds with good Sharpe ratios tend to have short track records or are invested in illiquid assets, where the volatility is essentially hidden (because prices move less frequently). The Aspect Diversified fund has achieved 17% annualised volatility between December 1998 and September 2007, similar to that of the stockmarket, but 15–20% annual returns.

Defenders of the sector argue that it does provide genuine diversification. Although managed futures funds do usually fall at market turning points (because they have been following the trend), they quickly adjust to falling markets.

Event-driven

Distressed debt

Distressed debt managers invest in bonds or loans issued by companies that are in trouble. Traditionally, they hope to exploit the fact that investors generally panic when companies look in danger of default, and that drives the bond price down to depressed levels.

It is a sector where managers often need a lot of expertise and a fair amount of stubbornness, fighting their corner against other classes of creditors when companies get into trouble. The distressed debt manager may feel he has spotted something in the documentation that gives him greater rights than other people suspect. Or he may parlay his position into equity rights in a restructured company, hoping there will be substantial upside.

Higgins says that managers in this sector "want to own debt that earns more than the cost of leverage and hope that the possibility of default is less than the market thinks". Ironically, thanks to their willingness to buy debt in troubled companies, they may prevent more companies from going into bankruptcy; in the old days, many companies would be in debt to banks, which would foreclose while they still had a good chance of reclaiming some value.

Merger arbitrage

Although this sector has an arbitrage label, it really is an event-driven approach. There is nothing that gets a stockmarket more excited than a big takeover. Not only does the share price of the target company shoot up, but the shares of other potential targets tend to rise in sympathy. Since the initial offer is rarely successful, investors eagerly await details of the second, higher bid or a rival offer from an outside group. Or perhaps the target company will try to buy investors' loyalty with a cash dividend or the spin-off of a division.

It is a situation that creates a lot of volatility, something that hedge funds love. And their interests tend to dominate when bids are announced. Twenty years ago, both predator and prey would have had to cultivate the big pension funds and insurance companies which were the long-term holders of the shares. But these days, such institutions are tempted to sell after the initial surge in the target's price; they would rather lock in a sure profit than risk losing out if the bid collapses.

If there is money left on the table, merger arbitrage funds try to exploit it. Higgins says:

> *If the deal were priced at $50 per share, mutual funds and*
> *pension funds would often get out at $49 because the upside was*

> *limited. But hedge funds would be attracted by that final dollar.*
> *With the use of leverage that can be turned into an attractive*
> *annualised return.*

Takeover bids, like other auctions, are subject to the "winner's curse" – the successful predator ends up paying too much. As a result, shares in the predator generally fall when a bid is announced, while those in the prey rise. So a simple merger arbitrage would be to go long of the shares in the prey and short of those of the predator. One academic study suggested that such a strategy would have delivered a return of 0.8% a month (around 10% a year) over the period 1981–96.

But this is another market that is highly competitive, since most hedge funds are following similar strategies. In the event, the funds are often betting on the bids going through, since if the deal fails, the shares in the prey will fall and those of the predator will rise (causing the hedge funds to lose money on both legs). They thus have an interest in pushing the target company to accept an offer. This may well lead to more takeovers occurring than happened in the past – a point that hedge fund critics (who worry about short-term pressures on company executives) are rapidly taking up.

Activist funds

The hedge fund group currently creating most of the headlines is activist funds. Their philosophy can best be summed up by a popular cartoon featuring two vultures. "Patience, my ass," says one vulture to another. "I'm going to kill something."

A classic example is the fund TCI, which took a stake of just 1% in ABN AMRO, a Dutch bank, and demanded action to break up the group and create value for shareholders. With such a small stake, the bank's management might have felt it could safely snub the hedge fund; certainly that might have been the case in earlier decades, when continental European companies felt free to ignore their shareholders. But within weeks, ABN AMRO was on the receiving end of a friendly bid from Barclays Bank, and then a more hostile (and ultimately successful) bid from the Royal Bank of Scotland.

The philosophy behind activist hedge fund investing is that company boards need to be pushed into action. Ruddick says:

*Sometimes you can spot an anomaly but you still need a
catalyst to turn that anomaly into a profit. Activist funds are the
catalyst.*

This can be an expensive process, since lawyers need to be used and
other shareholders canvassed. Other investors can also get a "free ride"
over the hard work done by the activists. One leading activist, William
Ackman of Pershing Square Capital Management, says:[7]

*Our preference is not to be activist if we can find a management
team that is already doing the right thing.*

However, there are also advantages. With a small stake, activists can
get a lot of leverage over executives, who may fear a shareholder revolt if
they do not act. Ackman says:

*What we do is akin to private equity, but we don't have to pay
an auction price, we don't have to use leverage and we don't
have to pay a premium for control.*

Traditionally, activists were seen as a force in the American market,
but they have been moving their attention to Europe. This helps explain
why they have been the subject of controversy; in continental Europe,
shareholders have traditionally been seen but not heard.

However, Guy Wyser Pratte of Wyser Pratte Investments says Europe
has some advantages for the activist:[8]

*In Europe, the activist manager has a captive audience in terms
of Anglo-Saxon fund managers who think the same way. Also
in Europe, the company bears the cost of a proxy battle, whereas
in the US it is the outside investor. And in Europe, shareholder
resolutions are legally binding; in the US, they are not.*

Finally, Wyser Pratte adds that in Europe, not many shareholders vote,
making it easier for an activist resolution to be successful.

An academic study[9] looked at the record of 110 activist hedge funds, mounting 374 campaigns in the course of 2004 and 2005. It found that activists typically targeted companies in the value stock category with low price to book or asset value and strong cashflows. There was a definite bias against targeting the largest companies, probably because of the cost of acquiring the initial stake. Around 40% of the cases involved a threatened shareholder vote, takeover or lawsuit and a quarter of all cases involved hedge funds acting as a block. On average, the campaigns resulted in improved returns for all shareholders.

Other funds

Hedge funds are ever inventive and there are some funds that do not fit plausibly into any of the above categories. Volatility arbitrage funds, for example, look at the fluctuations of different markets. If they expect volatility to rise, they might buy options that will rise in value. If they expect volatility to fall or be low, they will sell options (the equivalent of offering insurance).

Some strategies can be dubbed "alternative beta", in that they are not so much hedging as trying to exploit the potential for outsized returns in unconventional asset markets. One example is film finance. Traditionally, movies have been financed by the big studios or by banks; returns have been patchy, with most films failing to break into a profit and a few blockbusters making up for the rest. The big money has been made by the likes of Tom Cruise and Julia Roberts. Hedge funds have moved into this area, using various strategies: picking only low-budget films, or films in certain genres; or picking films that computer models suggest might be successful.

Other alternative beta approaches have included betting on footballers' careers, bankrupt power stations and weather derivatives. In some ways, the more obscure the asset class, the better. If few investors follow it, the chances are that prices will be set inefficiently and excess returns can be achieved. Furthermore, obscure assets are unlikely to be correlated with stock or bond markets.

Multi-strategy funds

Multi-strategy is a term that covers two distinct trends. The first relates to the managers. It makes sense for them to diversify their businesses, so many move from, say, convertible arbitrage into other strategies. As a group, they can thus be described as multi-strategy managers (many of those described in Chapter 2 fit into this category).

The second trend is for individual multi-strategy funds. For many of the strategies described earlier in this chapter there are periods when they are successful and periods when they struggle to earn decent returns. In an ideal world, investors would be able to anticipate those changes of fashion and would switch their funds accordingly. But even if they were blessed with perfect foresight, hedge fund investors would still find it difficult to transfer money because of notice and lock-up periods.

The idea behind multi-strategy funds is that they switch money on the clients' behalf. An asset allocator sits at the centre of the structure, deciding which strategies and which managers are likely to produce the best future returns. Because all the strategies are part of one group, the allocator does not have to worry about notice periods.

It sounds good, in theory, and multi-strategy funds could be a powerful competitor to the funds-of-funds groups (this issue is dealt with in Chapter 3). But it depends on two key assumptions: that the allocator gives money to the right people; and that the underlying managers are worth giving money to. Will you really get a team of superstars with this structure or merely a bunch of mediocrities? After all, the managers may be cheesed off if the allocator pulls money away from them; they may even be tempted to set up on their own.

There may be a cost advantage to clients, at least on the performance-fee front. In a fund-of-funds, the clients will end up paying performance fees to successful managers, but will get no discount from the underperformers. If half the managers outperform and half the managers underperform, the client may end up paying performance fees for mediocre returns. In a multi-strategy fund, there is just one performance fee for the whole fund. Having said that, the annual fees charged by multi-strategy managers can be high.

Whether or not they represent the best structure for clients, we may be heading for a world dominated by multi-strategy funds. It is now easier for new hedge funds to launch if they have the brand name of a big hedge fund attached. And although investors may doubt whether multi-strategy funds can be "all things to all men", it is easier to be credible if you already have a successful record (in some kind of strategy) than if you have no record at all. Successful hedge fund managers will gradually attract other funds, as a planet attracts satellites. Sometimes these strategies will be run as a bunch of separate funds. But the group may be tempted to offer a fund that groups together these strategies, as a kind of instant diversification package.

Ruddick says being a multi-strategy fund is a much better business model for the hedge fund itself. "Any fund that gets big enough will try to become a multi-strategy fund," he believes. For a start, moving into several strategies diversifies the manager's business risk; it avoids the risk that a single strategy will fail to work for a while. Furthermore, managers are often expected by clients to invest in their own funds; so developing several strategies helps to diversify their own wealth. This is all part of the convergence between hedge funds and the financial sector, the subject of Chapter 6.

2 The players

Most people will know the names of the big banks in their country; many will be aware of some of the big traditional fund management groups, such as Fidelity and Vanguard. But with the sole exception of George Soros, when it comes to hedge funds normal people will be stumped for a name. That adds to the hedge funds' air of mystery; but it may also increase suspicion in the minds of voters and politicians as these unknown souls earn a fortune for doing goodness knows what.

Worse still, managers come and go with remarkable rapidity. Vega Asset Management, a Spanish group, was hailed by some as Europe's largest hedge fund manager in 2004, but it made a series of bad bets on interest rates and currencies in 2006 and suffered a heavy hit from redemptions. Consequently, even those with an interest in investment can be stumped by a reference to "Joe Schmoe, the hot new hedge fund manager out of Acme Capital". So it is worth describing some of the more prominent names in the industry, as of mid-2007.

Some hedge fund managers like publicity; others go to great lengths to keep out of the public eye. Since they do not market their wares to the general investor, even their websites can provide little information. So, alas, it is not possible for this chapter to provide a comprehensive list; those not included have tried hard not to be so. And the length of the entries may well reflect the openness of the manager as much as the importance of the group.

AllianceBernstein

Only a small proportion of AllianceBernstein's near $800 billion of assets are managed in hedge fund form. But with $11 billion of hedge funds assets, that still puts the group in the industry's big league. Alliance moved into hedge funds in the late 1990s and follows what Drew Demakis, the co-chief investment officer of alternative investments, likes to call a "multi-alpha" approach. The funds follow long-short and market-neutral strategies across a range of assets including equities, fixed income, commodities and currencies; they steer clear of the arbitrage sectors. Demakis thinks the fund management industry will gradually "meld together", with hedge fund techniques being adopted by a wider range of investors.

AQR Capital Management

AQR was founded by four Goldman Sachs employees: Cliff Asness, David Kabiller, Robert Krail and John Liew. The group has a heavily quantitative-driven approach, derived from the Goldman years. Asness is a thoughtful writer about financial markets, being a high-profile sceptic about the dotcom bubble and campaigning against the "Fed model", a method of valuing shares on the back of Treasury bond yields. In 2007, Asness was ranked a hedge fund "brainiac" by *New York* magazine.

The group runs a range of portfolios, managing $35 billion in total as of July 2007, of which around $10 billion was in hedge funds. One of its hedge funds was hard hit by the market turmoil of August 2007, losing 12.5%, well outside the normal range of returns. That probably scuppered the chance of AQR's planned stockmarket flotation, at least in the short term.

Aspect Capital

This London-based managed futures group emerged like Winton (see below) from AHL (see the entry for Man on page 45). The founders include Michael Adam and Martin Lueck, the A and L of AHL. Its systems have a medium-term trend-following focus. As of July 2007, Aspect Capital had just over $5 billion under management; its flagship fund, Aspect Diversified, returned 12.8% in 2006. The group is attempting to build long-term relationships with a few key institutional clients.

Atticus Capital

This activist hedge fund is run by Timothy Barakett, whose brother Brett also runs a hedge fund group. Along with TCI (see page 51), the fund took a prominent role in opposing the purchase of the London Stock Exchange by the Deutsche Börse, its German rival. But to show Barakett had no hard feelings, he subsequently proposed that the Deutsche Börse should merge with Euronext, the Paris-based exchange. Atticus Capital, which makes big bets (railway stocks were one prominent example in 2007), had

$14 billion under management at the start of that year. Its flagship Global fund returned 35% in 2006.

Barclays Global Investors

The BGI group is best known for its index-tracking funds, which grew out of Wells Fargo's fund management business, acquired by Barclays, a British bank, in 1996. It is a quantitative-based house, although it prefers the term "scientific". The distinction, says Mike O'Brien, head of the group's European institutional business, is that the group "doesn't torture the data to death". That process can lead to discovering spurious statistical links. Instead, a market anomaly has to have a sound theoretical basis as well as a record of outperformance.

On the long-only side, BGI has successfully expanded its index-tracking business into "enhanced indexation", a process of making small bets relative to the index in a bid to produce outperformance at low risk. A move into hedge funds was the logical follow-through, and as of mid-2007 BGI managed around $20 billion in the sector. The group is also a big player in the provision of 130–30 funds (see page 99).

Brevan Howard

This was the first single hedge fund to list on the London Stock Exchange with an offering of its BH Macro fund. Its chairman was Ian Plenderleith, the man who handled the Bank of England's relations with the financial markets and a well-respected figure. However, in difficult market conditions, the launch was not the success it might have been, raising only €770m rather than the €1 billion it had targeted. Brevan Howard was set up by Alan Howard, a former bond trader at Salomon Brothers and Credit Suisse First Boston, and has specialised in bond and currency trading, earning a reputation for solid returns with low volatility. Its master fund had an annualised return of 10.5% between launch in April 2003 and January 2007. A secretive man, Howard attracted some criticism for failing to take part in the roadshow for the Macro fund flotation. But the fund still has its admirers. In October 2007, Swiss Re, an insurance group, took a 15% stake in it.

Bridgewater Associates

One of the biggest hedge funds in the world, Bridgewater Associates had

$30 billion under management in its Pure Alpha product (covering fixed income, equities, currencies and commodities) as at the end of 2006. However, hedge funds are only a small part of the operation; the firm had some $165 billion under management in total, with a largely quant-driven philosophy (see Chapter 1).

Its website makes Bridgewater sound like rather an alarming place to work. Founder Ray Dalio writes:

> *Substandard performance cannot be tolerated anywhere in the company because it would hurt everyone. Poor performance and/or uncooperative attitudes undermine the team. One of the most difficult responsibilities a team leader has is to cut poor performers, particularly those who are trying but don't have the ability. This is often perceived harsh or unkind, but it is ultimately best for everyone, including the person who is being cut. If you are thin-skinned and don't like conflict or criticism, you should be somewhere else.*

In 2007, *New York* magazine ranked Dalio as one of the "brainiacs" of the hedge fund industry.

Caxton Associates

One of the industry's pioneers, founder Bruce Kovner started in commodities trading, reportedly borrowing $3,000 on his credit card to speculate in soyabeans. He ended up, along with several other industry luminaries, at the Commodities Corporation, now part of Goldman Sachs.

Caxton Associates was established in 1983 and had $14 billion under management at the start of 2007. Kovner is a well-known supporter of conservative causes, and is chairman of the board of trustees of the American Enterprise Institute, a right-wing think-tank. After a fantastic run in the late 1990s, returns were reportedly modest in the first few years of this decade, although the flagship fund earned 13% in 2006.

According to *Forbes* magazine, Kovner earned $590m in 2006, making him the ninth best paid man on Wall Street.

Cerberus Capital Management

Cerberus was founded in 1992 by Stephen Feinberg, who previously worked at the now defunct junk bond house Drexel Burnham Lambert. Its initial focus was on distressed debt (junk bonds by another name). That led, fairly naturally, to an interest in investing in turnaround companies and thus into the private equity field.

The company has jumped into the public eye, first by recruiting luminaries such as former Treasury secretary John Snow and one-time vice-president Dan Quayle. Then it got involved in a series of high-profile deals, buying grocery chain Albertsons, the lending arm of General Motors, GMAC, and the car giant, Chrysler. Having bought the Japanese bank Aozora as well, Cerberus now has quite a diversified financial business. *Forbes* magazine says Stephen Feinberg earned $330m in 2006, and the *Financial Times* reported the group's assets at $16 billion as of October of that year.

Citadel

Citadel is one of the largest hedge fund groups with assets under management of around $12 billion at the start of 2007. At the time of writing, it had not floated on the stockmarket but it had raised $500m in a bond issue, a move widely seen as a trial run for a listing. Founder Ken Griffin started an investment fund at Harvard and then received backing from a Chicago financier, Frank Meyer. Citadel is seen as a highly flexible operator, swooping to buy a bankrupt mortgage lender during the early 2007 sub-prime crisis and making big profits in the energy market by picking up the energy positions of Amaranth, a struggling hedge fund, in 2006.

The group is also a classic example of the convergence of the financial industry. It has acted as a marketmaker in options, has a stock-lending operation (useful for other hedge funds that want to go short) and is planning to offer its back-office services to other hedge funds. Some people talk of Citadel as becoming the next Goldman Sachs.

But the heart of the operation is a quant-driven investment fund that buys and sells frequently on the back of computer models. Its largest fund, Kensington, produced annual returns of 22% over the nine years to the end of 2006. Griffin is gradually emerging as one of the more prominent managers of the young generation, donating money to a Chicago art museum and to prominent politicians. *Forbes* magazine's annual ranking of Wall Street's highest earners had Griffin earning $1.2 billion in 2006, placing him third on the list. He used some $80m of that to buy *False Start*, a painting by Jasper Johns.

CQS

A London-based hedge fund group, CQS specialises in arbitrage, covering convertible bonds, credit, and equities. It was set up in 1999 by Michael Hintze, who had previously worked at Credit Suisse First Boston special-ising in convertibles and equity derivatives. It managed to survive the problems that dogged the convertible sector in 2005. Assets under management had grown to $7.8 billion as of July 2007 and the group was running seven different hedge funds, as well as managing collateralised loan obligations (specialist funds operating in the debt markets).

Hintze takes great pride in his risk management systems and in the experience of his team, with the 46 portfolio managers having an average of 15 years in the business. Although the group uses quantitative models, Hintze is fond of saying that "a model is a great place to begin and a terrible place to end up". He is also well known for making a £2.5m loan to the Conservative Party and for having a gallery named after him and his wife at the Victoria and Albert Museum.

DE Shaw

One of the most successful quantitative-based funds, DE Shaw was estab-lished in America in 1988 by David Shaw, an academic from Columbia University (current professors can only dream of Shaw's reported $430m earnings in 2006), who helped develop Morgan Stanley's automated trading system. DE Shaw's original focus was on an equity market neutral strategy. Since then, it has added other hedge fund strategies, such as distressed debt and fixed income relative value.

The firm's forward march was interrupted in 1998 when, like other hedge funds, it lost a lot of money in the fixed income markets, causing severe embarrassment to a key lender, Bank of America. But it recovered swiftly and, with some $26 billion under management as of the end of 2006, *Absolute Return* magazine ranked it as one of the word's five biggest hedge fund groups. Lehman Brothers took a 20% stake in the group in March 2007.

DE Shaw has been one of the most prominent hedge funds to move into the long-only arena, setting up a specialist subsidiary, DE Shaw Investment Management, in 2005. It had already managed some long-only money for the state of Virginia's pension plan. In its new role, DE Shaw is competing with traditional quant managers such as Barclays Global Investors and Goldman Sachs.

In another example of "convergence" in the financial services industry, DE Shaw has a corporate lending subsidiary, Laminar Direct Capital, which lends to small and medium-sized companies. The company also owns one of New York's best-known shops, FAO Schwarz (a toy store), and has considered branching out into private equity. Shaw has recruited Larry Summers, former Harvard president and Treasury secretary.

ESL Investments

ESL is named after Eddie S. Lampert, who founded the company in 1988 with just a $28m stake. Lampert had previously worked for Goldman Sachs, leaving at just 25 to set up his own outfit. ESL has become best known for buying whole companies, notably K-Mart, a discount retailer, and later Sears, one of America's best-known shopping brand names. Lampert has modelled himself on Warren Buffett, arguably the world's most successful investor, who also started young and specialised in buying whole companies. Like Buffett, Lampert has a value bent, looking for companies he thinks the market has undervalued. At the end of 2006, ESL had assets under management of $17.5 billion.

Being kidnapped in January 2003 is part of the Lampert legend. Having snatched him from his office garage and tied him up in a motel bathtub, the criminals reportedly told Lampert they had been hired to kill him for $5m but would let him go for $1m. He persuaded them to release him if he paid them $40,000 two days later; when they came to collect the money, the kidnappers were arrested. After that experience, Lampert must find the odd bad day in the markets easy to cope with.

Farallon

Founded in March 1986 by Thomas Steyer, a Yale graduate, Farallon now has his alma mater (one of the most successful endowments in the world) as a client. Steyer worked at Goldman Sachs and then struck up a relationship with Hellman & Friedman, a private equity firm, which provided him with start-up capital.

Farallon is one of the largest hedge fund outfits, with $26 billion under management at the end of 2006, but also one of the most publicity-shy. It briefly hit the papers in a spat with American students, who accused it of an unethical investment policy in 2004.

Like Citadel, Farallon also attempted to take advantage of the sub-prime lending crisis in early 2007, extending a $200m rescue package to Accredited Home Lenders in return for warrants over the shares. The deal delivered only small profits when Accredited was acquired by a private equity group in May that year.

Farallon invests in a number of different strategies, including distressed debt, real estate, event-driven (company restructurings and spin-offs) and merger arbitrage.

Fortress Group

Fortress burst into prominence as the first big "alternative asset" manager to float on the New York Stock Exchange in February 2007. The listing was massively successful, with investors clamouring to get access to the small amount of stock that was on offer (less than 10% of the company), although the share price subsequently lost ground. Before the float, Nomura, a Japanese financial group, had bought a 15% stake in Fortress in November 2006.

Fortress was founded as a private equity firm in 1998 by Wesley Edens, formerly of the BlackRock fund management group, and Robert Kauffman and Randal Nardone, both from Union Bank of Switzerland (UBS). Assets under management grew sharply. At the end of 2001 the group ran just $1.2 billion, but according to the flotation prospectus, the company had just under $30 billion of assets under management as of the end of September 30, 2006. Only $9.4 billion of that was in hedge funds; the group's main area of business was private equity with $17.5 billion of assets. The hedge fund arm was divided into two parts, described as "hybrid" funds, investing in undervalued and distressed assets, and "liquid" funds, investing in the fixed income, currency, equity and commodity markets.

GLG Partners

GLG is a controversial British hedge fund group, thanks to several run-ins with the regulators. The group was yet another to be founded by Goldman Sachs refugees, Noam Gottesman, Pierre Lagrange and Jonathan Green, whose initials gave the company its name. The most successful fund was called Market Neutral and was run by a star trader called Philippe Jabre. But in 2006, both Jabre and GLG were fined £750,000 for alleged insider dealing (see Chapter 4 for more details). Jabre went on to start his own fund. Then, in 2007, the French regulator fined GLG twice for insider trading offences, and the SEC fined it more than $3.2m for earning illegal profits.

However, this tale of regulatory woe does not seem to have dented GLG's progress; it arranged a flotation on the US stockmarket via a deal with a shell company known as Freedom Partners. As of June 2007, it had more than $20 billion of assets under management.

Goldman Sachs

Many people have described Goldman Sachs as a hedge fund in disguise, because of the importance of trading to the investment bank's profits. But the group also runs hedge funds directly, such as the Global Alpha fund, and has a fund-of-funds operation to advise private and institutional clients. This has turned it into one of the giants of the industry, with more than $32 billion under management at the end of 2006.

The group has a heavily quant-driven style. However, 2006 was a difficult year, thanks to Global Alpha losing money and the fund-of-funds operation having a holding in Amaranth. The group's problems continued in 2007, with the Global Alpha fund losing 22.5% in August and a $3 billion "cash injection" being organised for another fund, Global Equity Opportunities. This injection was described as an "investment opportunity" rather than a bail-out and initially resulted in good returns for investors.

Leaving aside its own operations, Goldman Sachs seems to have given a start to half the hedge funds in this list. It is also one of the leading prime brokers.

Highbridge Group/JP Morgan

Highbridge was one of the first hedge fund groups to be acquired by an investment bank, with a controlling interest being bought by JP Morgan in 2004 for a reported figure of more than $1 billion. The purchase has been phenomenally successful, with funds under management growing from less than $7 billion at the time of acquisition to more than $33 billion as of March 2007. As a result, JP Morgan is perhaps one of the biggest manager of hedge fund assets in the world.

However, the initial omens were not good. One of Highbridge's main strategies was convertible arbitrage, which suffered horribly in 2005; the first quarter after the JP Morgan acquisition was the worst in the fund's history. But the fund rebounded and added new strategies in areas such as statistical arbitrage. JP Morgan has been able to channel the assets of its private clients (through its private banking arm) into the Highbridge stable; it also manages separately another $18 billion of hedge funds in areas such as real estate. Like other funds with a quant focus, Highbridge struggled in the summer of 2007; at one point in August, the group's statistical arbitrage fund was down 16%.

Highbridge was founded by Glenn Dubin and Henry Swieca, who met at the Wall Street group E.F. Hutton in the 1980s and set up the Dubin & Swieca asset management group. The duo initially specialised in the fund-of-funds market before establishing Highbridge as a separate group in 1997.

Kynikos Associates

Kynikos is one of the few successful short-selling groups. Founder Jim Chanos made his name spotting such duds as Enron. As with all short-sellers, he regularly courts controversy because companies dislike his activities, especially when he publicises his views in the media. In 2007, one of his targets was Macquarie Bank, an Australian investment bank involved in running and financing infrastructure projects around the world. Chanos's success in surviving for so long in such a brutal sector means that the wider investment community listens to his views with respect.

Lansdowne Partners

A London-based long-short manager, Lansdowne Partners has since branched out into global macro and long-only funds. It was founded in 1998 by Paul Ruddock, formerly of the Schroder fund management group, and Steven Heinz, who managed equities for Harvard University. The group is highly respected and was awarded the title of management firm of the year, in respect of its 2005 performance. Morgan Stanley paid $300m in 2006 for a 19% stake in Lansdowne. The group had $14 billion under management as of the start of 2007.

Long-Term Capital Management

The hedge fund that almost wrecked the financial system, LTCM was founded by John Meriwether, a bond trader from Salomon Brothers, who has since gone on to found another hedge fund, JMW Partners. A full account of the LTCM saga was given in Chapter 1.

Man Group

Arguably the largest hedge fund manager in the world with $61 billion under management as of the spring of 2007, Man was originally a commodity broker (E.D. & F. Man), which (among other things) was the sole supplier of rum to the British navy. It moved into hedge funds in the 1980s via the purchase of a stake in AHL, a CTA or managed futures group. The whole group was acquired in 1989.

Since then the Man Group has acquired Glenwood and RMF, both funds-of-funds managers, the first focusing on the retail market, the second on the institutional sector. It has also added Man Global Strategies, which seeds (makes initial investments in) new hedge fund managers. As of the spring of 2007, RMF had $25 billion under management, making it one of the largest funds-of-funds in the world; when it was bought for just $800m in 2002, it had only $8 billion under management.

Man's success has been built on its phenomenal ability to market hedge funds round the world which it attributes to its skill in financing intermediaries such as private banks and family offices. It has also been innovative in launching new products, notably guaranteed funds such as the MAN IP 220. This seems to have persuaded investors to venture into the world of hedge funds (a field many intrinsically regard as risky) by promising them, at worst, that their money will be returned.

Man has gradually focused on its hedge fund activities, selling off its commodity side and, in 2007, spinning off its futures brokerage business. The group has increased its public profile via its sponsorship of the annual Man Booker Prize for fiction (it has recently added an international and an Asian prize to the stable). It has also reflected ex-chief executive Stanley Fink's interest in climate change by sponsoring an international climate change award and Global Cool, an initiative aimed at reducing carbon dioxide emissions by 10 billion tons.

Marshall Wace

London-based Marshall Wace has one of the more interesting business models. The idea stemmed from a discussion of the value of advice from the "sell side" (investment banks and brokers), which pumps out hundreds of stock recommendations every day. Marshall Wace did some analysis to see whether trades based on these recommendations would be successful; the answer was yes. The development of the internet meant it was possible to systematically collect and analyse that information, and in 2001 Marshall Wace duly launched its Tops product.

Tops is a long-short portfolio, which uses the best ideas generated by the salesmen who work at the banks and brokers. Salesmen talk every day to the analysts who follow individual stocks and sectors and then pass the best of those ideas on to clients (the buy side) that deal in the market. The salesmen have every incentive to come up with good ideas since they are paid on commission; the better those ideas perform, the more trading will be allocated their way.

It might seem that this model could be easily replicated. After all, the investment banks pass their ideas on to a whole range of clients, not just Marshall Wace. Other fund management groups could do the same thing or, even worse, investors in Marshall Wace could get the brokers' recommendations directly and cut out the middleman.

Some rival funds have indeed been launched. But Paul Marshall, one of the firm's two eponymous founders, says these days the fund's alpha is largely generated from the way the ideas are mixed together, rather than from the raw recommendations. And with its market power (as of March

2007, it had $12 billion under management), the group will always have access to the best salesmen.

The success of the model means that, apart from the banks themselves, Marshall Wace has become the largest trader in the European markets, with 5% of daily volume. In autumn 2006, Marshall Wace floated one of its Tops funds on the Euronext stockmarket.

Moore Capital Management

Another graduate of the Commodities Corporation, Louis Bacon set up Moore Capital Management in 1989, giving the group his mother's maiden name. An early bet against the Japanese market and in favour of oil prices went extremely well, and in its first year the group made 86%. It was hit hard in 1994, when bond markets suffered badly, and reportedly lost 90% of its clients. But it bounced back with a 25% return in the following year. The group is one of the most successful and long-lasting global macro funds, with $12.5 billion under management at the start of 2007. It is a secretive group, with a website that gives no information to outsiders; fees are reportedly 3% of assets plus 25% of profits.

NewSmith Capital Partners

NewSmith was founded by ex-Smith New Court and Merrill Lynch employees such as Michael Marks, Paul Roy and Stephen Zimmerman, men with long-established reputations in the London financial markets. As of the end of April 2007, it had over $7 billion under management. The group has extensive operations in Asia as well as long-short funds, managed out of London, covering Asia, global equities and credit; the last-named was given the title European Credit Fund of the Year in 2006. In 2005, *Hedge Fund Review* magazine gave NewSmith the title Hedge Fund Group of the Year. The group also has a financial solutions division, which advises clients on complex financial products such as credit derivatives.

Och-Ziff

Dan Och was a merger arbitrage specialist at Goldman Sachs who set up a hedge fund in 1994, with the backing of the Ziff brothers, who had sold their publishing firm to a private equity group, Forstman Little. In a speech given at Wharton University in 2005, Och recalled that on his first day, the firm had one employee, a telephone and a lamp.

Och-Ziff expanded from merger arbitrage to become a multi-strategy manager, running money in convertible arbitrage and event-driven sectors. It also runs private equity and real estate funds. In Britain, the company is perhaps best known for providing some of the financing for Malcolm Glazer's takeover of Manchester United.

The group's master fund had delivered annual returns of 17% after fees by July 2007, when the group announced plans to float (and raise up to $2 billion) on the New York Stock Exchange. It had nearly $27 billion under management as of that date. According to *Forbes* magazine's annual ranking of Wall Street's highest earners, Och was the 19th highest paid individual in 2006, with earnings of $300m.

Pershing Square Capital Management

Pershing Square is an activist hedge fund spearheaded by William Ackman, who previously was a co-founder of Gotham Partners, a group that closed down amid a flurry of lawsuits. Ackman has continued to court controversy since then, launching campaigns to target management strategies at Wendy's and McDonald's, for example, as well as a long-running campaign about the accounting practices at MBIA, an American insurance giant.

Renaissance Technologies

Renaissance is one of the most successful systematic trading funds, a style that uses computers to exploit small anomalies in the market. Led by Jim Simons, a prize-winning mathematician, the group has a heavily science-based ethos, hiring PhDs rather than Wall Street traders, and working from a "campus" on Long Island.

In a speech given to the International Association of Financial Engineers in May 2007, Simons modestly said:

> There is no real substitute for common sense except for good
> luck, which is a perfect substitute for everything.

He started his trading career, making directional bets on commodities, with just $600,000. He bought sugar at 20 cents a pound and the price quickly reached 60 cents. The fund grew by a factor of ten within a year.

Simons started to develop his systematic style in the 1980s, launching the Medallion fund with just $25m in 1988. Within five years, the fund was closed to new investors, the classic sign of success. The fund also became notorious for charging the highest fees around, namely 5% annually and 44% of all profits. Investors were happy to pay those fees because of the fund's phenomenal record; its worst year reportedly showed a gain of 21%. In 2005, Simons returned all outside investors' money and ran the Medallion fund only for staff members.

But this was the prelude to the launch of a new fund, Renaissance Institutional Equity, for which Simons publicly targeted $100 billion. This was an ambitious target, but by May 2007 the fund had already attracted $26 billion. Fees – at 1% annually and 10% of profits – are much lower than for the Medallion fund and the style is different. Rather than the high-frequency trading that marked Medallion, the fund is looking at longer-term factors, including fundamentals such as company balance sheets. However, like many other quant-based funds, Renaissance was caught up in the August 2007 turmoil, with its main fund losing almost 9% in a few days.

Simons has used his wealth to encourage the development of maths teaching in America and has funded research to find the causes of autism, from which his daughter suffers.

SAC Capital Partners

SAC takes its name from its founder Steven A. Cohen, who has followed perhaps the classic success story of a hedge fund manager. Originally from Long Island, Cohen became a junior trader on Wall Street after college and ended up running a trading group at his firm, Gruntal. Like many traders before and after him, he set up on his own in the 1990s, eventually expanding into running a multi-strategy operation.

Among the strategies being followed are long-short equity, convertible arbitrage and statistical arbitrage. Cohen's success can be judged by his ability to charge a 50% performance fee (rather than the traditional 20%) on his funds, although this figure is only taken after a hurdle rate. The group's flagship fund returned a remarkable 34% in 2006. In July 2007, SAC announced talks on the sale of a 20% stake to outside investors.

Cohen has come into the public eye for his extraordinarily high income and for his activities in the art market. He was about to buy Picasso's *Le Rêve* from casino owner Steve Wynn, when Wynn put his elbow through the canvas. But he did manage to purchase Willem de Kooning's *Police Gazette* for $63.5m. *Forbes* magazine's ranking had Cohen as the second highest earner on Wall Street in 2006, with $1.2 billion, and he certainly does not seem shy about spending it.

Soros Fund Management

For a long time the biggest name in the industry, Hungarian-born George Soros has kept in the public eye, thanks to his political and philanthropic activities. He is a keen enthusiast for open societies in eastern Europe and a strong opponent of the Bush administration in America. He also regularly opines on global issues and fancies himself as something of a philosopher manqué, having written several books.

For a long time, his Quantum fund was seen as the template for hedge fund activities, making big bets on currencies and markets, notably gambling against the pound in September 1992. Soros has a market theory called reflexivity, which roughly states that perceptions shape the fundamentals. When banks perceive the risk of lending against assets to be low, speculators will be able to borrow money and buy property, pushing up prices and reinforcing the banks' willingness to lend. Some unsuccessful bets in the late 1990s caused Soros's record to lose a bit of its lustre, but the group still had $11 billion under management as of the start of 2007. The fund is now largely in the hands of Soros's sons, Robert and Jonathan.

Steinhardt Partners

Not the first hedge fund group, but one of the pioneers, Steinhardt, Fine, Berkowitz & Company was set up in 1967 with less than $8m in capital. Early success in the go-go markets of the late 1960s (the fund returned 99% in its first full year) was followed by the ability to make money (by going short) during the bear market of the mid-1970s. The other founders dropped out and the firm was renamed Steinhardt Partners in 1979.

Steinhardt had an aggressive trading style, investing largely in equities but also in currencies and bonds (which gave him a problem in the final years of his fund). After a difficult 1994, the fund was closed down in

1995. In his autobiography *No Bull,* he said that "a great deal of our success came from getting the markets' overall direction right". Steinhardt was also one of the earliest firms where casual dress was encouraged; as Steinhardt put it: "I persuaded myself that walking round in pullovers and Bermuda shorts would somehow ameliorate the pressure."

Steinhardt was one of the big beasts of the hedge fund era, not as well-known as Soros but with a similar record – he achieved returns, net of fees, of 24% a year for 28 years. Any investor who stuck with him to the end would have become exceedingly rich. He is now critical of the industry, arguing that "it's all about making money for the managers"; his management fee of 1% a year was designed to cover expenses, so it was only the performance fee that earned him real money. This, he believes, was a true alignment of interest between investors and managers.

TCI, or The Children's Investment Fund

The long version of the company's name reveals an important part of its purpose. Founder Chris Hohn ensures that a significant portion of the group's profits is devoted to charity. The charity, run by Hohn's wife, Jamie Cooper-Hohn, helps children throughout the world, particularly those with HIV or AIDS. It benefits from an automatic fee of 0.5% of funds under management every year and gets a further 0.5% if the return is higher than 11%; that worked out at £230m for the year ended August 31st 2006.

Hohn combines reticence about his personal life with an aggressive public approach, since TCI is an activist hedge fund. Its first high-profile campaign was against the takeover of the London Stock Exchange by its German equivalent, the Deutsche Börse; not only did Hohn succeed in blocking the deal, but the German's group chief executive, Werner Seifert, was forced to resign. Another prominent target was Dutch bank ABN AMRO, at which Hohn successfully campaigned for a sale on the back of a stake of just 1%. Before setting up TCI, Hohn had followed an activist style at Perry Capital, an American hedge fund group.

Third Point Capital

This activist hedge fund group is run by Daniel Loeb, who is known for his aggressive letters complaining about the chief executives of companies he perceives as underperforming. He described one such executive as having an "empire-building philosophy, pathological selfishness and poor business judgment". He feels strongly about executive perks, such as limousines and expensive sports tickets.

Third Point Capital, established in 1995, had gathered nearly $7 billion of assets by June 2007. It listed its main fund in London in July that year (on the back of an average annual return of 23%, after fees), although it raised only €380m rather than the €500m that had been hoped for. Loeb reportedly paid $45m for a Manhattan apartment near Central Park.

Tiger Fund

One of the big beasts of the hedge fund industry's early years, Tiger was a macro fund founded by Julian Robertson in 1980. Its most prominent early success was calling the turn of the dollar in 1985. Ironically, one of its later mistakes was underestimating the strength of the dollar in the late 1990s. Robertson also bet against the survival of the dotcom bubble. Redemptions prompted him to close the fund in March 2000, just as his bet against technology stocks was about to be proved right. Several Robertson employees, known as "tiger cubs", have gone on to found successful hedge fund groups of their own, such as Stephen Mandel of Lone Pine and Lee Ainslie of Maverick Capital.

Tudor Investment Corporation

Paul Tudor Jones is from Memphis, centre of the American cotton industry, so perhaps it was no surprise that his first foray into financial markets was as a cotton trader. In 1980, he became a local on the commodities market, trading on his own behalf. He set up Tudor Investment Corporation in 1983 and was smart enough to predict (and profit from) the 1987 stockmarket crash. Indeed, he had lived up to the absolute return aim of the hedge fund industry, having never (as of 2007) had a down year. However, one of Tudor's funds, Raptor, was caught up in the turmoil of August 2007, suffering unexpected losses.

Tudor Jones is not renowned for his willingness to talk to the press, but in a 2000 interview he said that the secret of a successful trader was to achieve an annual return two or three times the biggest drawdown (fall in fund price). He also said that he used a combination of technical analysis (looking at charts) and fundamental analysis to generate returns.

Tudor Jones was one of the first prominent hedge fund managers to get involved in charity work, establishing the Robin Hood foundation, which attempts to fight poverty in New York City via educational grants and job training. He is also an enthusiastic supporter of wildlife conservation. According to *Forbes*, he earned $430m in 2006.

Winton Capital

Winton is a CTA, or managed futures, group with more than $9.5 billion under management as of June 2007. Founder David Harding was the "H" in AHL, the CTA that was eventually bought by Man Group, and became one of the cornerstones of that group's successful move into the hedge fund industry. Harding (whose middle name is Winton) left the group to set up his own firm in 1997. Winton claims a compound annual return of 19% since launch and has established a second fund, Evolution, which can invest in assets other than futures, such as equities and swaps. The company has set up research campuses in Oxford and Hammersmith, west London, to encourage work in statistics and actuarial science. In October 2007, a fund run by Goldman Sachs acquired a 10% stake in the Winton group.

3 Funds-of-funds

Hedge fund fees are high enough to raise questions about whether they make more money for themselves than for their clients. But that is not the only problem for potential investors. Most access the sector via a fund-of-funds manager, which charges a further layer of fees on top. All told, investors could end up paying 3% of their money each year even before the effect of performance fees. That is a big hurdle to overcome.

So why do investors bother? Two factors are probably most influential:

- The time and expertise needed to analyse a range of sophisticated hedge fund strategies. Such costs might easily equal the extra fees paid to a fund-of-funds manager, at least when an investor is in the process of setting up a hedge fund portfolio. One academic cites $50,000 as the cost of due diligence on an individual hedge fund.[1] Or, as an investor put it: "There are no yellow pages for hedge funds."
- The comfort blanket a fund-of-funds manager can provide. At the very least, investors should expect the manager to spot the fraudsters. They might also expect him to avoid those funds that were taking excessive risks – hence there was some disquiet when it transpired that both Goldman Sachs and Man Group's RMF arm had held money with Amaranth Advisers. But for those managers who avoided Amaranth, the crisis was a godsend; it will have discouraged many institutional investors from trying to pick funds themselves.

The danger of fraud means there is a need for funds-of-funds to be pretty well diversified. Academic research suggests the optimal portfolio would consist of 10–15 hedge funds. But Dan Higgins of Fauchier Partners says that does not allow for the operational risk that a manager could blow up; if that happened in a portfolio of only 12 hedge funds, an entire year's returns could disappear. As a consequence, Fauchier aims for 20–25 funds.

Few private investors have the capital to create a diversified portfolio of hedge funds on their own, even if they had the ability to do so. Few pension funds want to make their initial foray into the sector with a single fund, lest some bad numbers taint their whole experience. So funds-of-funds managers are an important force behind the expansion of the industry. By March 2007, Hedge Fund Research reckoned that funds-of-funds managed assets of $684 billion, more than 40% of the industry's total funds under management.

It is an industry that is dominated by the Europeans. *Absolute Return*'s October 2006 survey had Man as the largest fund-of-funds group, followed by UBS, Union Bancaire Privée, Permal, HSBC, Société Générale, Credit Suisse, Julius Baer, Crédit Agricole and Grosvenor Capital Management. Apart from Permal, which is owned by Legg Mason, an American group, and the Chicago-based Grosvenor, the others in the top ten are all based in Switzerland or the European Union.

As is usual in the hedge fund world, there are no definitive statistics. Hedge Fund Research says there were just 80 funds-of-funds in 1990 and 2,307 by the end of June 2007. In contrast, a study by Ibbotson Associates found that the number of funds-of-funds had risen from 98 in January 1995 to 991 in October 2006.[2] Over that period, the mean size of their assets had risen from $250m to $3.5 billion. The biggest fund-of-funds back in 1995 had just $800m under management; by 2006, that had risen to $23.4 billion. At that time, most funds-of-funds controlled assets of between $50m and $1 billion, although there were a few with less than $1m, which seems rather hard to imagine.

The Ibbotson study found that, up to a point, performance improved with size while volatility tended to decline. The smallest 25% of funds underperformed the largest 75% by around 2 percentage points a year.

Why might this be? The largest managers are probably well-established, have better research staff and will have access to the best fund managers – access that might not be available to the individual hedge fund client. This is one of the main selling points of the sector.

However, the academic evidence that value is added by funds-of-funds is rather mixed. A study by academics Harry Kat and Sa Lu found the average manager underperformed an equally-weighted portfolio of hedge funds by almost 3 percentage points a year.[3]

More discouraging figures were found by William Fung and Narayan Naik, professors at London Business School. They co-authored a paper that showed the average fund-of-funds delivered no alpha (after fees) over the periods 1994–98 and 2000–04.[4] There was a brief era, ironically after the collapse of Long-Term Capital Management in 1998, when managers delivered a lot of alpha, around 11 percentage points a year. The collapse of LTCM meant that risky assets were cheap and a lot of hedge fund managers made big profits by betting on a reversion to the mean.

Over the period 1994–2003, Fung and Naik reckon only 21% of fund-of-fund managers created alpha. And things got worse; during 2004–05, the proportion of alpha managers fell to 5%. In other words, you had a one-in-20 chance of finding a manager with skill.

The only good news from this study is that there did not appear to be any managers with negative alpha – in other words, those people whose decisions actively reduced the value of the investor's portfolio. But Fung and Naik reckon this is because such firms do not last long; investors quickly desert them and they go out of business.

At the moment, few pension funds would feel happy about selecting a hedge fund manager directly, or indeed concentrating their exposure to the sector on just one or two managers. However, once pension funds get used to the sector, they may be willing to abandon the fund-of-funds route, rather as a toddler eventually lets go of its parent's hand. "Pension plans that got into funds-of-funds five years ago now believe they can do it themselves," says Sorina Givelichian of Russell Investment, a consultancy group.[5]

How funds pick managers

Analysing hedge funds is a sophisticated process. One approach is to spot the factors that are driving returns, such as the level of the S&P 500 (the main stockmarket index on Wall Street) or the change in bond yields. This is the underlying approach of many hedge fund clones (see Chapter 6). Omar Kodmani of the fund-of-funds group Permal says:

If you throw enough factors at something and use multiple

regression, you will always find some explanation. We
think a more meaningful approach is to use, say, 80% of the
performance data and then find the factors that explain that.
Then we apply those factors over the other 20% to see if it still
fits.

Kodmani thinks that three or four factors explain the performance of most hedge funds.

Permal was founded back in 1973 when, as Kodmani says, there were many fewer hedge funds to choose from. The group has more than doubled its assets under management over the past five years. "We have to spend a lot of time explaining how we can still outperform even though we have grown," admits Kodmani. Its largest fund has returned 11% a year since Permal started to manage it in 1995.

David Smith is chief investment director of the multi-manager group at GAM (part of the Swiss group Julius Baer), responsible for the fund-of-funds range which had $26 billion under management as of May 2007. Smith says:

We have a bottom-up, labour-intensive research driven approach.
We like to visit every single hedge fund and reach a level of detail
which makes me feel comfortable. We like to sit and ask exactly
how the funds operate and come back every quarter to see if
they are still operating that way.

This drive for perfection has led Smith to develop his own statistics for the industry, surveying everyone he can think of for details of the funds in existence.

In building a fund, Smith will establish its desired characteristics in terms of expected returns, volatility and correlation with the market. The asset allocations to different types of funds flow from those characteristics. The key, he believes, is manager selection. "All the time I am looking to see if the funds we have selected are beating the sector average, after fees," he says.

This detail-driven approach makes Smith no respecter of reputations. When he first joined the firm in 1998, he redeemed his holdings in 80%

of the group's managers, including George Soros and Julian Robertson. He says:

> We analyse all our redemptions and we found that a third go out
> of business within 12 months, a third underperform and a third
> outperform. So we get about two-thirds right.

A different approach is taken by Man Global Strategies (MGS). It looks for early-stage managers, starting their first hedge funds, with the hope of benefiting from their growth. The process is known as seeding. Alex Lowe, the group's chief executive, says the group saw around 700 of the 1,500 hedge funds launched in 2006. Of these, it did due diligence on 80 and then whittled that down to 15 for investment approval. Man then used its own capital to fund these start-ups for 6–9 months to see how they performed; around one-third dropped out at that stage, largely because they were not doing "what it said on the tin". Funds that passed all those stages would then be moved into clients' portfolios.

The result of this process, says Lowe, is that after two years, the group will have a good idea of how the hedge funds work. Their funds will have been run on a managed account basis, enabling MGS to see the daily positions taken by the manager. If all goes well, MGS will try to take the manager up to the next stage; in one successful example, San Francisco-based Bayswater, which MGS seeded with $25m in 2004, was running $660m for Man alone by July 2007.

Another company in the Man Group, RMF, starts from a different premise. Having divided the industry into five buckets, such as relative value and directional (see Chapter 1), it constructs a diversified portfolio, making sure that each bucket has at least 10% and not more than 35%. The individual managers are then rated on a series of criteria, such as operational risk, with only the best qualifying for consideration.

Fauchier Partners is a fund-of-funds group that is 50% owned by BNP Paribas Asset Management, a French group. It runs around $4.5 billion of assets, with around half coming from other asset managers (such as Cazenove) and private bankers. Its best known fund, Paragon Capital Appreciation, has a stable track record, delivering 8% annual returns (with 6% volatility) since its foundation in August 1995.

The group says it makes no attempt to time the direction of markets but aims for a balance between absolute value strategies (such as macro and equity long-short) with a few specialists such as merger arbitrage and volatility arbitrage funds. It avoids funds with excessive leverage or black box funds, where the source of alpha is not clear.

The outlook

The danger for funds-of-funds may lie in excessive risk aversion. They will be desperate to avoid backing the next Amaranth or Bear Stearns, so they will go for stable hedge fund managers. The result may be modest returns that, after fees, are unexciting. Someone who feels the industry has already gone down that route is Ken Kinsey-Quick of Thames River Capital:[6]

> *The returns have been bland because not enough risk has been taken, as the fiduciary responsibility has been paramount due to the institutionalisation of the industry.*

Thames River, which runs both individual hedge funds and funds-of-funds, is accordingly aiming for more innovative funds with higher returns.

One way of avoiding the blandness problem is for fund-of-funds managers to slice up the industry, offering funds based on strategies (distressed debt, equity long-short) or geography. In a way, they are following the tradition of the mutual fund industry, which developed to offer the Baskin-Robbins model of a variety of investment flavours, from emerging markets to corporate bonds.

Funds-of-funds can be viewed in a mixed light by hedge fund managers themselves. They are, of course, a vital source of assets. But they can also be a lot more fickle than pension funds or individual investors. When they want to switch money out of a hedge fund, this can be a problem for a manager with a sophisticated strategy, even when that manager has a lock-up period. If the forced sale of assets adversely affects performance, other fund-of-funds managers may be tempted to pull out, resulting in a downward spiral that could eventually lead to the closure of the fund.

However, funds-of-funds face their own liquidity dilemma. Often, they may offer their investors monthly liquidity (albeit with a notice period). But they may be investing in hedge funds that have quarterly liquidity (and a quarterly notice period) and in start-up funds that have a lock-up period of a year or more. Then there are gating arrangements, clauses in hedge fund agreements that allow the managers to restrict the level of redemptions. This can be based on a proportion of the fund or on a proportion of an individual investor's holding. Combine a 10% gate, and quarterly redemption, and it could take the fund-of-funds 30 months to redeem its holdings.

So what happens when investors in the fund-of-funds want to redeem their holdings? The temptation for the fund-of-funds manager will be to get rid of the most liquid of the underlying funds, regardless of their performance. Another possibility would be to borrow money to meet redemptions. But if redemptions are occurring in a skittish market, this might entail taking on risk at the worst possible moment; the remaining investors could be adversely affected.

Structured products

Another way that investors can have a "safe" hedge fund investment is to buy a structured product. This usually combines an investment in a hedge fund, or fund-of-funds, with a guarantee. The idea is to entice investors who might otherwise be nervous about the risks (of fraud or otherwise) of investing in the hedge fund sector.

The guarantee will usually be provided by what is known as constant proportion portfolio insurance or CPPI. The bulk of the investor's capital is invested in zero coupon bonds or their equivalent; these will grow steadily to pay back the capital at the end of the product's life. The rest of the portfolio is invested in hedge funds. The proportions are not set in stone but managed continuously; if the hedge funds perform well, they are allocated more capital; if they perform badly, more money will be invested in bonds.

While these products undoubtedly have commercial appeal (Man Group, in particular, has been successful in selling them), they have several drawbacks:

◪ The guarantee is in nominal, not real, terms. If you get just your money back after five years, with no allowance for inflation, you will have suffered a real loss.

◪ The guarantee applies only at the end of the period; if you redeem halfway through the product's life, you may not get your money back.

◪ The way that CPPI works means that if hedge funds do suffer a sharp loss, all the fund's money could be moved into zero coupon bonds quite quickly. You could then be sitting on dead money for several years.

◪ The fees involved can be huge. As well as those charged by the manager (or the fund-of-funds manager), there can be an initial fee by the product issuer of 1–2% plus annual guarantee fees.

But the final point is more philosophical. Hedge funds are supposed to be about delivering absolute, not relative, returns, thus reducing risk. Funds-of-funds should reduce the loss of risk further. So adding a guarantee on top of this structure is belt-and-braces, with Velcro as well. It seems an unnecessary encumbrance.

Multi-strategy versus funds-of-funds

The growth of the funds-of-funds sector shows no sign of slowing down. But there is a long-term potential threat to their position. Multi-strategy funds offer many of the same services as funds-of-funds groups, giving investors a diversified portfolio covering a range of different strategies. Sometimes they have a star manager in charge that can attract investors. Perhaps they could replace funds-of-funds in the long run.

As mentioned in Chapter 1, multi-strategy funds have one potential fee advantage over funds-of-funds, linked to the netting of performance fees. The net effect should be better for clients. However, while this effect sounds good in theory, in practice, multi-strategy funds are known for charging pretty high fees.

Furthermore, funds-of-funds feel obliged to offer reasonable liquidity terms to investors. But, according to Howard Berkowitz of the BlackRock group (and a partner in one of the earliest hedge funds), "the liquidity in multi-strategy funds is getting worse all the time."[7]

There are plenty of challenges, but the funds-of-funds sector seems likely to continue its growth. Fred Siegrist, chief executive of RMF, says:

> *The fund-of-funds business will develop into a two-tier market. On the one hand, many smaller boutique-type providers will continue to sell specific themed products and operate profitably in niches. On the other hand, a number of highly organised big providers will provide a wide product range to fulfil all clients' requirements. In the middle, between the two models, asset managers will find it hard to survive.*

This is a perfectly plausible assessment, although it is also exactly the kind of forecast that commentators make about most industries: that only the giants and the niche players will survive. The bizarre thing about the fund management world is that struggling managers can be only one good year from success, while established managers can be just one bad year from disaster.

4 Hedge fund regulation

Hedge funds have grown so fast, made so much money for their principals and had so much effect on the financial markets that they have naturally attracted the attention of the world's regulatory bodies. Rarely a year goes by without some kind of official report being issued on the sector.

The world is split into two distinct camps on the issue. Let them alone, say regulators in free-market Britain and America. Tie them down, say politicians in continental Europe. The free-market camp has normally won the day, for the simple reason that hedge funds are globally mobile; unless all countries agree to restrict their activities, they will move to the region that gives them the greatest freedom.

In May 2007, Germany tried to push fellow finance ministers at a G8 meeting to agree a code of conduct for the industry, but faced resistance from the Anglo-American camp. Following the meeting, the German finance minister was reduced to the pious hope that a code would emerge "spontaneously" and "voluntarily" from the industry.

The Germans did have one good point. The speed of growth of the industry, its specialised nature and its peculiar client base (few small, or retail, investors) mean that regulation has turned out to be a bit of a mess. A survey by the International Organisation of Securities Commissions (IOSCO) in March 2006 found, for example, that no regulator had adopted a formal, legal definition of the term "hedge fund".[1]

It would be a mistake to think that hedge fund managers want no truck with the regulators at all. They recognise that low standards can keep potential investors away. Stanley Fink, deputy chairman of Man Group, says:

> We are generally very pro-regulation. It keeps the cowboys out
> of the industry and we much prefer a situation where the law is
> clear and rules can be followed.

There is, however, an intrinsic tension between regulation and the concept of hedge funds. Hedge fund managers have established themselves to escape from the paperwork that dogs their long-only counterparts. They want to keep their positions secret so that others cannot trade on the back of them. But this worries continental European politicians, who want markets to be as transparent as possible, so that hedge funds cannot build up large stakes in secret. However, Callum McCarthy, chairman of the UK regulator, the Financial Services Authority (FSA), said in December 2006:[2]

> We do not seek, nor would we find it useful to have information about specific large positions of individual funds or their managers.

What are regulators worried about? There are three main issues. The first is fraud – that investors may be ripped off. The second is that hedge funds, in their eagerness to earn performance fees, may break the rules by, for example, trading on inside information. The third is that hedge funds, either by overreaching themselves (borrowing too much) or by all making the same bet, could destabilise the financial system and, by extension, the economy.

In terms of fraud, the most common response has been to limit the kind of investors who can buy into hedge funds, on the grounds that more sophisticated investors can perform their own assessment (or pay someone to do it for them). In terms of market abuse, the same rules apply to hedge funds as to anyone else (although the authorities are worried that hedge funds might gang up to force companies to accept a takeover; such collusion can be devilishly hard to prove). And on systemic risk, the main focus has been to look at the overall level of borrowing, to avoid a repetition of the LTCM saga.

Approaches to supervision

But there are a number of potential approaches to supervising the industry. Some countries impose restrictions on what hedge funds can do. For example, in Portugal the use of derivatives is controlled, whereas in France there are limits on leverage. In Russia, the authorities' attitude is even more robust: Bill Browder, the founder of Hermitage Capital, a specialist in Russian investing and forthright critic of some local corporations, was barred from entering the country after November 2005.

In America, the president's working group on financial markets, which reported in February 2007, took the line that the industry should be regulated by looking at the banks and prime brokers that deal with hedge funds; the best way, the group hoped, of ensuring a hedge fund failure does not lead to systemic risk.

The most common approach, according to the IOSCO report, is to regulate the advisers, the people who manage the hedge funds. The idea is that this should offer investors some protection against outright fraud, but of course it does not stop them from losing money if the manager's strategies prove unsuccessful.

Britain

Britain's FSA has followed this route, and to date the British hedge fund industry has been pretty free of scandal.

Observers say the FSA appeared to approach the industry in a sensible way. One prime broker says:

> They took the view that they didn't know enough, but they did regulate the investment banks and the hedge funds were our clients.

So the FSA conducted a survey of the prime broking sector and got some aggregate data on its exposure to hedge funds, first on a voluntary and then on a mandatory basis. That should help the regulator spot the emergence of another LTCM, by giving a warning of when leverage levels are getting excessive. The prime broker says:

> We think the FSA has gone from thinking that hedge funds are the root of all evil to being comfortable now they have all the facts.

The most publicised FSA action involved GLG, one of Britain's leading hedge fund groups, and its star trader Philippe Jabre. The case involved the issue of securities by Goldman Sachs in a Japanese company, Sumitomi Mitsui Financial Group. Jabre was told about this issue in advance, a situation known in the jargon as "crossing the wall", being aware of confidential information. He sold the shares short and made a profit because the issue of the new securities was deemed by the markets to be bad news for the share price. The FSA fined Jabre and GLG £750,000 apiece.

Given the frantic trading activity of hedge funds, this is bound to be a big area of regulatory interest in future. The French authorities have worried that hedge funds will collude in an attempt to push companies into being taken over; there has also been concern that hedge funds will use contracts for difference, a kind of geared bet on prices, to build up stakes in secret.

Another step that the FSA has taken is to warn about the use of "side letters", provisions that give certain favoured investors special terms. Such terms may include lower fees or a shorter notice period. The FSA did not want to block side letters, but it did want to ensure that other clients knew about such arrangements; after all, the favoured clients will be in a privileged position if the fund gets in trouble and they can make a swift exit.

America

Up until now, the American regulatory touch on hedge funds has been extraordinarily light. (An exception is the managed futures sector, which is regulated by the Commodity Futures Trading Commission.) For a long time hedge funds were not even registered in their role as advisers, thanks to a loophole in the law that did not require registration for advisers with fewer than 15 clients. The law was interpreted as to count each hedge fund as a single client (even though the fund may have had dozens of underlying investors). Thus an adviser looking after 14 hedge funds, with assets worth several billion dollars, might not need to register because of a law designed to exempt Mom-and-Pop advisers in small towns.

The Securities and Exchange Commission (SEC), America's regulator, attempted to move down the FSA route by imposing a rule that all hedge fund advisers should register with the commission by February 1st 2006. Almost 1,000 advisers signed up to register, although some could escape the rule by imposing a two-year lock-up on investors. (This would have had the perverse effect of giving less protection to investors with the least liquid holdings.) But the SEC ruling was struck down by an appeals court ruling in June 2006, which argued that the regulatory body did not have the authority to oversee the sector, especially as the term hedge fund was not mentioned in American securities laws.

The key piece of American legislation is the Investment Company Act of 1940, which has been used to regulate traditional fund managers. Hedge fund managers have used two strategies to get round the act: the first is to limit themselves to fewer than 100 investors; the second is to recruit only highly sophisticated investors. The effect is to limit clients to the very rich or the institutions.

For a long time (ever since 1982), the definition of a rich person for the purposes of the 1940 act has been someone with an annual income of $200,000 or $1m in assets. However, house price inflation meant that an awful lot of people were starting to meet the $1m test. So in December 2006, the SEC voted to raise the minimum to $2.5m, excluding the value of an individual's main residence. At the time of writing, this change had yet to be approved by Congress and hedge fund lobbying may prevent it from happening (although the president's working group recommended the rule be adopted). If the rule does go through, the effect, according to a Wolters Klouwer study, will be to cut the number of eligible investors by 88%.

The quid quo pro for this light approach is that the SEC imposes severe restrictions on the way funds can be marketed. It says that hedge funds cannot attract investors through, among other things:

> ... *advertisements, articles, notices or other communications placed in a newspaper, magazine or similar media, cold mass mailings, broadcasts over television or radio, material contained on a website available to the public or an e-mail message sent to a large number of previously unknown persons.*

This is one reason hedge funds are often shy about talking to the press; they do not want to be perceived as marketing their funds to the wider public.

It cannot really be said that the record of supervision of American hedge funds has been a great success. In September 2005, for example, the founder and chief financial officer of the Bayou hedge fund group both pleaded guilty to conspiracy and fraud charges. Their crime was to inflate the performance of the fund, with the aim of attracting new investors and persuading existing investors to retain their holdings.

Harry Davis and Sahar Shirazi of Schulte Roth & Zabel, a law firm, recount the story of one manager, John Whittier, of Wood River Partners, which had $265m under management:[3]

> Whittier failed to have any audits conducted, had no independent administrator to review the fund's holdings and valuations, kept the fund's portfolio secret from all but a few employees, and failed to make regulatory filings that would have disclosed its highly concentrated holdings in one smallcap stock called Endwave.

The IOSCO report noted:

> [In America] the growth in hedge funds has been accompanied by a substantial and troubling growth in the number of fraud enforcement cases – most notably involving hedge fund advisers. Hedge fund advisers were also key participants in recent scandals involving late trading and inappropriate market timing.

One problem may be that hedge funds are much more established in America and are thus more appealing to rich investors than they are to Europeans, who are still cautious about the industry. Fink says:

> Most of the scandals in the US concern fraudsters who just happen to have perpetrated their fraud through the hedge funds sector.

But it is hard to spot frauds until after they have happened. As the SEC's 2003 study said:[4]

> The Commission typically is able to take action with respect to fraud and misconduct only after it receives relevant information

from third parties and frequently only after significant losses have occurred.

The SEC brought 51 hedge fund fraud cases between 2000 and 2004. A particular problem is valuation. The SEC report said:

> *The broad discretion that advisers have to value assets and the lack of independent review over that activity gives rise to questions over whether some hedge funds' portfolio holdings are accurately valued.*

This is hardly surprising. The incentives for advisers to lie are strong. After all, if performance is poor, investors will withdraw their money. The adviser will not just lose the annual management fee on those assets; he could lose his job if the fund becomes uneconomic to run. And if returns have been only moderate, an extra kicker to valuations could ensure a juicy performance fee for the manager. The IOSCO report found that eight of the countries it surveyed had developed specific policies for valuation, such as involving another party (for example, the custodian bank).

Other approaches

One potential answer is self-regulation. Together with IOSCO, a voluntary industry body called AIMA (the Alternative Investment Management Association) published a *Guide to Sound Practices for Hedge Fund Valuation* in March 2007, suggesting steps such as the appointment of an independent valuation service provider, the use of multiple price sources, and the disclosure of any material involvement by the manager in the production of a fund's net asset value (NAV). Certainly, it is highly unlikely that any serious institution would consent to give money to a fund manager without receiving strong assurances about an independent approach to valuation, custody and auditing.

However, there is a fundamental difficulty when it comes to complex instruments, such as derivatives. These instruments may well be traded "over-the-counter", rather than on any recognised exchange. There may not be a market price available. And the instruments may be so complex that no outside party can match the expertise of the hedge fund manager.

In such circumstances, the best that independent valuers and investors may be able to achieve is to understand the models that the manager is using to price the assets.

The laissez-faire attitude of regulators towards hedge funds may come under pressure as less sophisticated investors get involved with the sector. This may happen as hedge funds launch "permanent capital" funds directly on the stockmarket. Or it may happen with the regulators' active encouragement. After all, it is hard to see why private investors should not own hedge funds, which mostly control risk carefully, when they were allowed to buy technology funds, some of which lost 90% or more of their value after the bursting of the dotcom bubble.

In March 2007, the FSA published a paper on funds of alternative investment funds, or FAIFS, which was aimed at making it easier for retail investors to own hedge funds.[5] In a bumper helping of alphabet soup, these funds will operate under the NURS system. NURS stands for non-UCITS retail schemes and UCITS, in turn, stands for undertaking for collective investment in transferable securities. It is hard to understand why simplifying a system can sound so complicated.

Fink has some worries about opening up the industry to the small investor:

> Most sales have to go through intermediaries and they want to be paid 1% a year. If your minimum holding is £25,000, then the intermediary will get paid £250 a year for a few years, enough to get to know the client properly. But if you're dealing in lots of just £1,000, then the fee will be just £10.

He doubts whether an intermediary would be prepared to do a proper risk assessment of the client for that sum.

Hedge fund structure

Tax and regulations means that hedge funds have to adopt a rather peculiar structure to get round the rules. The first step is to establish the holding company in an offshore centre that is "tax neutral", a euphemism for saying that no tax is charged. Typically, this will be Bermuda or the Cayman Islands. This holding company will hold all the assets.

The holding company will be the centre of the wheel; spokes will lead from it to the other parts of the structure. Typically, there will be a master fund, and then at least two feeder funds that invest in it. The first, for onshore investors in America or Britain, will be a limited partnership; again, the partnership will have no tax liability since the authorities will "look through" it and tax the investors directly. (Sometimes, funds are organised as limited liability partnerships. The tax effect is normally the same; investors avoid paying two sets of taxes.) The second will be an offshore feeder fund, designed for foreign investors and those (such as pension funds) that are tax-exempt.

This offshore holding company will have its own directors. It is they who will appoint the hedge fund managers and will have the right to hire and fire them. They will receive the management fees and then pass them on to the manager, after taking their cut. The key, says Robert Mirsky, practice leader, hedge fund services at Deloitte, is that the only decisions made by the fund manager concern which securities to trade. This independence is crucial to maintain the beneficial tax structure.

But this structure is really based on a fiction. When a manager wants to launch a hedge fund, he can go out and recruit some independent directors; there are firms that specialise in the business. They are hardly likely to hire anyone else to run the fund or indeed to fire the manager, since investors have subscribed to the fund on the basis that this particular manager is running it.

If the manager concerned is a boutique operator, there may be another spoke in the wheel: a marketing company that recruits investors in return for a commission. A hedge fund will also need the help of probably six other professional services to operate: an accountant and a lawyer to set up the structure; an auditor; an administrator, who will deal with matters such as reports and accounts; an independent valuer, who will advise on pricing illiquid securities; and a prime broker.

As well as pooled funds, a hedge fund manager may also offer a managed account to investors. In these cases, the investor gives the manager a discrete sum of money and delegates the decisions on how that money should be invested. However, the account is transparent and the investor is always aware of the manager's holdings and the trading decisions he is taking.

Managed accounts can give the investor a lot of reassurance. But as one industry veteran admits, "They're a pain in the neck to run." As a result, big managers don't want to touch them. Small management groups will accept them as the only way of getting assets; medium-sized firms will accept them only if the account is large enough to make up for the hassle.

Prime brokers

Prime brokers are the key intermediaries and the people that some regulators are relying on to act as their eyes and ears for the hedge fund industry. The brokers are departments of investment banks that act as service providers to the hedge funds, a sort of combination of butler and accountant. Indeed, prime brokers can also act as midwives, since one of the services they offer is that of start-up consultancy, helping tyro managers to find office space, hire staff and get the technology that they need to run their business. Goldman Sachs, Morgan Stanley and Bear Stearns are generally seen as the leading brokers; a survey by Lipper Hedge World in 2006 found that, between them, they controlled almost 60% of hedge fund assets.

Prime brokers provide a range of services including the clearing and settlement of trades, the monitoring of positions and custody (investors usually insist that the assets of the fund are held in a separate place to reduce the scope for fraud). But the money that investment banks make from acting as prime brokers generally takes three main forms. The first is lending stock to hedge funds so they can take short positions; the banks charge a fee for doing so. The second is lending money so the manager can use leverage in the fund to enhance returns. The third is a so-called ticket fee, which applies if the hedge fund uses someone other than the broker to make a transaction. Prime brokers can get away with this last charge because they provide a consolidation service for funds, keeping track of the trades they make and the positions they have taken.

Many hedge fund managers have more than one prime broker. This is particularly the case for multi-strategy funds that trade lots of different types of securities. It will also be important if the hedge fund trades in exotic, or over-the-counter, securities that are not traded on a public market; such securities can be difficult to move from one bank to another (although the situation is improving).

Furthermore, investment banks have many potential conflicts of interest when dealing with hedge funds: their trading desks are buying and selling in the same markets; they may be advising on takeovers or new issues in which the hedge funds are dealing; they may also be suggesting to clients which hedge funds to back. Information about the hedge funds' positions would be useful to all those other operations. So having more than one prime broker is a way for hedge funds to protect themselves.

One prime broker says:

> Clearly, with prime brokerage, we get to see everything a client does. If clients were to suspect that information found its way to our traders, we would be out of business in a day.

As a result, banks have "Chinese walls", designed to stop the prime brokers from passing information to, or even fraternising with, the rest of the staff.

Nevertheless, big hedge funds are reluctant to take the risk of relying exclusively on one broker. "A bit of healthy competition keeps the brokers honest," admits one leading player. However, there is a limit. Some hedge funds went as far as getting five or six brokers and found it too much of a hassle to monitor all those relationships; they are cutting back to two or three.

Prime brokers may make a lot of money from hedge funds but they are also taking plenty of risk. If the hedge fund goes bust, it may not be able to repay the money it has borrowed. As a result, the prime brokers demand collateral when the hedge fund manager takes out a loan; this is usually in the form of a claim on the assets of the fund.

Hence it is in the interest of the prime broker to be sure that those assets are being valued accurately. One prime broker says:

> I don't want a hedge fund client to overvalue its assets. I want its securities to be marked accurately so I can sleep at night.

A classic example of this occurred in June 2007 when Bear Stearns, a

Wall Street bank, revealed it had problems with two of its hedge funds that had investors in securities linked to the sub-prime mortgage market in America. Falling house prices and poor lending standards meant that many of those loans were struggling and the Bear Stearns funds were losing money.

Bear Stearns had raised some $2 billion from investors for its two funds, than borrowed another $10 billion via prime brokers to gear up their returns. So naturally that was a problem for the brokers when things started to go wrong. They asked for more collateral. Bear Stearns came up with a proposal that it would pump up to $3.2 billion into the funds, provided the banks refrained from making further margin calls for an extended period. The brokers turned down the deal and one of them, Merrill Lynch, started to sell off the collateral on its books.

This was a high stakes poker game. If the hedge funds did not have enough money to cover their debts, the prime broker had a natural interest in realising as much money as possible, as quickly as possible. But a fire sale of the hedge funds' assets would simply drive down the prices of the assets concerned. Some of those assets might be held by Merrill Lynch (or by other hedge funds, for which Merrill acted as prime broker). So the result might have damaged Merrill's long-term financial position. In the end, a compromise was reached; Merrill auctioned off only part of its collateral, and Bear Stearns agreed to put up cash without conditions.

Note, however, that Bear Stearns was not offering to bail out the investors in the funds, only the prime brokers. (Eventually, investors in one of the funds lost all their money.) That indicates where the power really lies. For Bear Stearns to operate on Wall Street successfully, it needed the goodwill of the other big investment banks.

The saga also raised two interesting points. First, the fact that Bear Stearns felt obliged to put its own capital at risk to bail out the funds indicates why regulators need to keep a watchful eye on the sector. One day, a hedge fund could bring down a leading Wall Street firm. But the second, and contrasting, point is that the firms concerned managed to sort out the problem without any input from a regulator.

Of course, prime broking is not the only way in which hedge funds interact with investment banks. They can use a bank as the administrator (the person who makes sure all the paperwork is correct). The bank also provides the hedge fund with research, suggesting which securities are the best to buy. "Hedge funds are the best customers of investment banks," says Nicholas Roe, European head of equity finance at Citigroup. The relationship was once even cosier. As Patric de Gentile-Williams of PCE Investors says:

> It used to be the case that brokers would provide managers with free office space in return for trading commissions but that's not allowed any more.

Nevertheless, Dresdner Kleinwort has estimated that hedge funds earn around $50 billion a year for the investment banking sector. That does raise the question of whether they can really be the effective watchdogs for an industry that pays them so well.

Managing their own risk

The more sophisticated hedge funds take risk seriously. After all, they do not want to go out of business because of a mistake in assessing the volatility of their portfolios. Pat Trew is chief risk officer at CQS, a London-based hedge fund manager. He points out that managers face four distinct types of risk. The most obvious is market risk (that prices move against you), but there is also liquidity risk (an inability to sell your positions or have the right level of margin on a leveraged portfolio), counterparty risk (that the firm you trade with fails to pay up) and operational risk (which covers anything from valuing positions incorrectly to failing to comply with regulations).

Trew has accordingly developed what he calls the "seven pillars of risk assessment", which he uses to subject the funds to a series of stresses, including the time it would take to offload the vast bulk of a fund's portfolio. He says:

> You have to consider whether the portfolio is appropriate given the duration of your capital and the depth of the market. The worst scenario is to be a big player in a market that deteriorates rapidly and every investor wants out.

cQS also has over 30 people in its information technology and operations departments. The latter is responsible for confirming that transactions are processed as accurately and smoothly as possible and has played its part in industry forums, such as the IOSCO working group on valuation. Its basic philosophy is that hedge funds are paid to take risk in the markets, not in their operations and how they run their business.

Some of this work could be outsourced, of course, but risk control is something that the funds-of-funds groups and the consultants who advise hedge funds take very seriously these days.

Just because little has gone wrong so far does not mean it cannot go wrong in future. In particular, regulators worry that brokers might be exposed because hedge funds are making the same bets, and that asset classes that appear to be unrelated might become so in a market sell-off (see also Chapter 5). A Financial Stability Forum report in May 2007 said:[6]

> [Intermediaries should be looking to improve] their measurement
> and their ability to aggregate exposures across the firm's
> activities, improve margining and collateral management
> practices, and improve stress testing practices, especially
> regarding market liquidity risks.

Regulators would like to see both hedge funds and prime brokers use "stress tests" to work out what might happen if things go wrong. But part of the problem with stress tests is the tendency to base them on events that have happened in the past. However, the next crisis is rarely like the last. The Financial Stability Forum report worried whether:

> ... firms take sufficient account of low probability events that
> would impose very large losses on them and other market
> participants. Internal incentives may work against firms taking
> full account of such events in limit setting, capital charging and
> other risk management policies.

In other words, if hedge funds or prime brokers take too cautious a view, they will miss out on the chance for profit. And profit can translate into some juicy bonuses.

One potential weakness is the use of value at risk or VAR models. These try to assess the maximum amount a portfolio can lose in any short period; inevitably the assessment is based on past data (which can prove misleading). When volatility is low, VAR models provoke firms into increasing their capital-at-risk, only to cut it when volatility increases. But if everyone is using these models, they will all want to sell when volatility spikes, a process that will push volatility up even further. That sounds like a recipe for crashes.

All told, the Financial Stability Forum report concluded:

> Areas of continuing weakness in many funds have been identified. These include: pricing and valuation of illiquid securities; analysing market correlations; lack of stress-testing, absence of concentration limits, overreliance on statistical value-at-risk measures; inadequate tracking of liquidity; insufficient use of electronic platforms and the need to further standardise industry documentation.

In particular, the report said that smaller managers and those who had not attracted institutional investors had not developed their risk controls. The industry still has plenty of work to do.

5 Hedge funds: for and against

Hedge funds attract some pretty strong opinions. A friend of the author, someone who has spent an entire career in investment management, described them as "a menace; they're not interested in the business or in the long term at all". Trade unionists and left-wing politicians express their concern in much more graphic terms.

The case against hedge funds comes in three distinct varieties. The first is political, and is closely linked with the general case against free-market liberalism. At its heart, hedge fund critics simply dislike the ability of managers to make so much money and worry that this is made at the expense of ordinary people. In their eyes, hedge funds are simply the latest example of rapacious capitalists, from a long line that includes multinational corporations, investment bankers and private equity groups. Resentment is particularly high in continental Europe, where hostile takeovers and active shareholders are recent innovations.

Similar arguments were made against the corporate raiders in the 1980s and were outlined by Will Hutton in his book *The State We're In*.[1] Hedge funds destroy rather than create; they are interested in short-term profits and not the long-term health of a business. They push companies to return cash to shareholders, or to get taken over. That stops executives from investing in new plant and equipment, or from taking on new employees; indeed, hedge fund actions seem to result in a loss of jobs.

The second variety of criticism focuses on the risks that hedge funds take. As this book has made clear, hedge funds are only lightly regulated; the positions they take are not open for analysis by outsiders; they can also use borrowed money to enhance returns. In the case of LTCM, they used an awful lot of borrowed money and the Federal Reserve started to worry about the stability of the financial system. With even more hedge funds around today, is the financial system even more at risk?

The third type of criticism centres on the deal that investors receive. Hedge fund fees are too high in a world of low nominal returns. They may ensure that managers get rich, but the same will not be true for the clients. It is a rewrite of the old Wall Street tale about a trainee who is taken to the harbour; he is shown the hedge fund managers' yachts and then the yachts of the prime brokers that serve them. "But", asks the naive youngster, "where are the customers' yachts?"

The role of hedge funds in society

It certainly seems hard to claim, at first sight, that hedge funds earn rewards commensurate with their contribution to society. Doctors, firemen and policemen all perform roles that appear much more useful.

So how can a case be constructed in their favour? Hedge funds provide liquidity to the market, and thus make it easier for businesses to raise money. Indeed, they may well lower the cost of capital. And to the extent that business finds it easier to grow, more people will be employed and society will be more prosperous. If that is worth, say, $20 a year to each person in the United States and Europe, it adds up to $10 billion to be shared around by the hedge fund managers.

This line of reasoning may sound like special pleading from a free-market fundamentalist. But think, for a second, about risk and insurance. In a world without insurance, companies would rapidly go out of business if their factory burned down. By pooling together risks, insurance companies play a valuable role in society; they make it easier for businesses to be established and to survive.

Financial risks may be less obvious but can be just as damaging as physical ones. Exchange rates may move in the wrong direction, interest rates may soar, plunging stockmarkets may deplete a company pension fund. These risks can be parcelled up and dispersed, just like the risk of fire and theft; hedge funds play a part in this process. By adding liquidity to the markets, they make it easier and cheaper to insure against those risks.

Peter Bernstein says in his book *Capital Ideas* that "because the stockmarket makes diversification easy and inexpensive, the average level of risk-taking in society is enhanced".[2] We need only to look at countries where it is hard to set up businesses because of regulation or corruption to realise the benefit of more open societies.

A cynic might still say, "Well, where is my $20?" It is probably made up of a small amount of incremental gains; lower prices from a company here, better employment opportunities there, and better, or more efficient, services somewhere else.

If that argument seems a little contrived, the subject could be approached from the opposite direction. What would the world be like if we banned hedge funds from operating? The process would involve a lot of government interference. To regulate fees, the authorities would have to prevent a client from entering into a commercial arrangement with a fund manager. And if they stopped clients from paying hedge funds too much, why not lawyers, accountants or footballers?

We could attempt to cap the incomes of individual hedge fund managers by taxation. But the era of high taxation (an effective 98% rate in Britain in the 1970s) was hardly an economic golden age. The same tax rate would catch other successful people and be a disincentive to work hard.

This is not to say top tax rates could not be higher than they are at the moment; there is always room for argument at the margin. However, in an era of labour mobility, any one country could not push its tax rate too high without driving a lot of business abroad. So any attempt to cap hedge fund incomes would need to be co-ordinated at the global level. After all, there would be high incentives for any country to undercut the others, so as to attract all those rich people. This is why so many hedge funds have their nominal headquarters in the Caribbean. Taxing financial transactions more highly would run into the same problem, and would undoubtedly raise the cost of doing business for everyone.

Another approach would be to restrict what hedge funds could do by, for example, banning short-selling. But, as was argued in the Introduction, short-selling plays an important role in setting prices accurately. Or we could try to restrict the ability of hedge funds to get involved in takeovers by imposing a minimum holding period before investors could use their votes. Again, we would expect investors to demand a higher return for buying shares with restricted rights; in other words, the cost of capital would go up. It is far from clear that countries that restrict the ability of companies to be taken over end up more prosperous as a result; all that results is complacent executives who milk the company for benefits rather than pursue the best interests of shareholders.

Protecting national champions from takeover sounds superficially attractive. But think about the British car industry, which is churning out a lot more cars through Nissan, Ford and General Motors than it would surely have done under the old British Leyland. Or take the financial services industry itself, Britain's most important industry. Quite a lot of it is in foreign hands but the result is that London is challenging New York for the title of premier global financial centre.

Industry protectionism leads to higher prices for consumers, since the result is local monopolies. It also prevents economies from benefiting from the process of creative destruction, as capital is reallocated from inefficient businesses to more efficient ones. Hedge funds give this process a helpful shove.

An academic study, already cited in Chapter 1, which looked at the actions of activist hedge funds over the period 2004–05, found no support for the view that hedge funds destroyed value or were short-term in focus.[3] It found that campaigns run by activist funds resulted in abnormal returns for investors and focused on companies with a low price to book, or asset, value. The highest returns occurred when the sale of the company was targeted; hostile approaches were more successful than friendly ones.

Hedge funds and risk

When the dotcom bubble was at its height in 1999–2000, American retail investors piled into technology mutual funds and British investors bought technology unit trusts. Within three years, several of those funds had lost 90% of their value. Yet few people talk about the riskiness of the mutual fund industry.

This is the sort of thing that frustrates hedge fund enthusiasts. After all, their industry spends a great deal of time trying to control risk. The head of the FSA, the UK's regulator, estimated that just 0.3% of funds collapse every year.[4] But a few examples (Long-Term Capital Management or the 2007 near wipe-out of two Bear Stearns credit funds) taint the whole industry.

However, we have to recognise that risks have to be taken to generate any return that is greater than cash. Hedge funds are not completely hedged. International Asset Management, a funds-of-funds group, has a nice definition:[5]

It is better to think of a hedge fund as a fund that hedges away any risk not related to its speculative strategy.

The risks that concern regulators about hedge funds are threefold. The first, as highlighted in the last chapter, is the problem of fraud. As institutions become more involved in assessing hedge fund managers, checking their backgrounds and monitoring their systems, this problem should be reduced. The second is the scope for market abuse; it should be possible to adapt existing rules to cope with this problem.

The most important risk is the question of leverage. Although not all hedge funds use leverage, the concept is inherent to the industry. Traditional long-only equity managers have a great advantage; the market normally goes up, quite often delivering double-digit annual percentage returns. If a hedge fund manager properly hedged, it would be hard to match that kind of return; the gap between their long and their short positions is not likely to be that wide. But provided their skill is real and persistent, the managers can use leverage to gear up their returns so they are competitive with the market, and can justify their fees.

This use of leverage means that hedge funds can be a lot more important to the system than their assets under management would suggest. When LTCM wobbled in 1998, the fund's positions were so large that most of the big banks were potentially affected. The Federal Reserve, America's central bank, was worried that the markets would freeze, as institutions worried about the health of those they traded with. That was the problem that led the Fed to organise a rescue; a central bank should not normally worry about hedge fund investors on the basis that they should be able to look after themselves.

Ever since the LTCM saga, central banks have made it their job to try to monitor the relationship between banks and hedge funds. The April 2007 issue of the Bank of England's financial stability report, for example, contained a two-page section on hedge funds and financial stability. Its conclusions were reasonably benign, pointing out that the market easily coped with problems faced by the Amaranth hedge fund in 2006. However, it added:

Amaranth's failure occurred at a time when financial

market conditions were generally benign. In more adverse circumstances, fire sales of assets could have been more dangerous and the impact wider.

A Financial Stability Forum report concluded:[6]

Since the LTCM crisis, risk management practices and capacity at core intermediaries have been substantially enhanced. Prudential supervision has been strengthened and become more risk sensitive. Risk management capacity at the largest hedge funds has also improved, driven in part by increased institutional investor interest.

The report added that the exposure of the big banking groups was "modest in relation to their capital".

Indeed, on balance, the evidence has been that hedge funds have played a pretty benign role in the system. They have taken risk off the hands of the banking system, and in the past it has been banking failures that have turned recessions into depressions.[7] If a hedge fund or two goes bust, a few investors will lose part of their portfolios, but there should be no wider impact provided they are not using the kind of leverage favoured by LTCM.

One worry is that hedge funds might herd and all take the same positions. The summer of 2007 suggested three examples:

1 The problems experienced by quant funds - the managers who use computer models to select stocks. Although their models may be sophisticated, they all tended to analyse the same data. The result was that many bought "value" stocks, those that looked cheap relative to their peers on the basis of a few financial ratios, and those that had "momentum", in other words had been rising in price. When the quant funds decided to cut their positions, they all had to sell the same stocks. Their models went haywire as their carefully diversified portfolios suddenly seemed a lot more correlated than they should have been.

An early academic study of the episode[8] suggested that the "systemic risk in the hedge fund industry may have increased in recent years". The study added:

> A co-ordinated withdrawal of liquidity among an entire sector of hedge funds could have disastrous consequences for the viability of the financial system.

2 The ownership of structured products – sophisticated instruments constructed from pools of assets. Some of those assets were mortgage-linked securities. When it became clear that some of those securities might default, nobody wanted them. Hedge funds needed to cut their positions to reduce risk, but they could find no buyers. The sector was effectively making a bet on illiquid assets, a bet that went wrong when liquidity disappeared. (Of course, some hedge funds profited by betting the other way, but they were a minority.)

What made life even harder was that the new instruments were hard to value. As the Financial Stability Forum report commented:

> The greater complexity of financial risk intrinsic to recent structured credit and other product innovations poses challenges in risk management and monitoring even for the most sophisticated firms and risk managers. It has become more difficult to understand the risk profiles of firms and of the financial system as a whole.

These assets are also "securitised" – that is, previously illiquid assets that have been bundled up and sold in packaged form. As well as mortgages, such assets include credit card loans and car loans. Securitising these loans takes them off the banks' books, which seems like a good thing for the financial system as a whole. But what if that knowledge alters lenders' behaviour? After all, if you know you are stuck with a loan, you will make sure the borrower can repay it; if you can sell it on, you may be less scrupulous. Clearly, lax lending standards lay at the root of the sub-prime mortgage crisis.

There may be a natural incentive for hedge fund managers to buy illiquid instruments. Given that they trade infrequently, the prices of such assets are less volatile for long periods than traditional investments such as shares or bonds. Many managers are judged on the basis of the Sharpe ratio, which compares returns to volatility. Buying illiquid assets improves this ratio, at least in the short term.

3 **The "carry trade"** – the borrowing of money in currencies with low interest rates to fund positions in currencies or assets with higher yields. The dollar was the vehicle of choice for the carry trade in the early part of this decade, thanks to American rates of just 1%. But since 2004, the yen has been used more regularly. The carry trade is highly attractive for hedge funds because it normally yields a positive return every month because of the interest rate differential.

In the long run, the carry trade ought not to work, and indeed the evidence suggests it does not over periods of ten years or so. This is because a high yield on a currency is generally compensation for the perceived risk of depreciation. Think of how John Major and Norman Lamont battled to save the pound in 1992 by raising interest rates, but investors still gambled successfully that sterling would devalue. So there is a risk that the small gains made from the carry trade could be wiped out in one big move (in this case, rather than a devaluation, it might be a surge in the yen).

How serious are these combined risks? In 2007, the New York Federal Reserve warned that correlations between different hedge fund sectors had been rising, just as they had before the LTCM crisis in 1998.[9] Tobias Adrian, author of the New York Fed's study, wrote:

> *If the returns of many funds are either high or low at the same time, the funds could record losses simultaneously, with possible adverse consequences for market liquidity and volatility.*

In short, if all the funds have similar positions, they may have no one to sell those positions to in times of crisis.

The big threat was that all the risk might return to the banks. After all, just three prime brokers were linked to 60% of the hedge fund sector's assets. The banks also earned vast fees for putting together the structured products and the securitisations the hedge funds bought. Without those fees, the financial sector, a big employer in America and Britain, might look a lot less healthy.

Investor returns

The last area of criticism of the industry (but one that has received a lot less media attention than the other two) is the idea that the average investor has received, or will receive, little benefit from owning hedge funds. Perhaps managers are not given the right incentives. Performance fees are assumed to align the interest of managers and investors. But do they encourage managers to take too much risk on the grounds that they will become extremely rich if the bet pays off, whereas if it fails, they will still have the comfort of the annual fee?

The evidence suggests this is not an insoluble problem. First, managers usually invest their own money alongside that of their clients. Second, if they have had a bad quarter, clients will withdraw their funds; they have limited patience for losses. Indeed, some investors feel hedge funds are taking too few risks these days. Michael Steinhardt, one of the industry's pioneers, said:[10]

> If I made 11% in a year, I'd be committing hara-kiri. These guys make 11% in a year and they're overjoyed.

That feeling has been given added weight by the generally lower level of returns in the 2000s than in the 1990s. To take one example, the MSCI Investable Hedge Fund Index returned just 3.2% in 2004, 4.7% in 2005 and 7.3% in 2006, not much better than cash.

The industry's supporters say this criticism is overstated. Omar Kodmani of Permal says:

> Returns have fallen since the 1990s but so has volatility. On a risk-adjusted basis, hedge funds are still doing well.

Academics have spent a lot of time looking into this issue. Their first argument concerns the indices that are used to illustrate hedge fund performance. Simply put, indices are believed to overstate returns. This is because not all hedge funds make it into the data throughout their existence. Some may simply choose not to report their figures, or may cease reporting them; often this is because their performance is poor. This survivorship bias is accompanied by backfilling; managers get into the indices only if they have a track record of a couple of years. Funds that cease trading within those first two years (again, usually because they do not produce great returns) will not make it into the indices.

A study by Roger Ibbotson and Peng Chen found that, over the period 1995–April 2006, these biases could make an enormous difference.[11] If backfilling and survivorship bias were allowed, the annualised return looked like 16.5% a year. If both factors were excluded, the return dropped to 9% a year. In other words, statistical biases accounted for almost half the return. But other studies find a smaller number; 2% a year was the figure quoted for the 1994–2001 period.[12] *What does this mean?*

Then there is the problem that the most successful managers tend to close their funds to new investors. This is because they do not want their funds to become so large that their returns are diluted (and their performance fees reduced). As a result, the index providers produce two types of indices: investable and non-investable. The latter have generally produced much better returns than the former. Potential clients will be misled if they think they can match the returns of the non-investable indices.

Finally, the indices cover quite different segments of the hedge fund universe. William Fung and Narayan Naik took the databases of five different providers; they found that only 3% of hedge funds were common to all five. In the case of three of the five providers, some 15–20% of the hedge funds analysed were unique to their database. In short, these indices do not relate to the hedge fund industry in the way that the S&P 500 and the FTSE 100 relate to the American and British stockmarkets.

For whom the bell curve tolls

There are also criticisms about the way that the hedge fund returns are generated. Harry Kat (now a professor at City University Business School, previously at the University of Reading) analysed the statistical properties of the returns.[13] Naturally occurring phenomena usually have a normal or bell curve distribution, with most measurements grouped together in the middle. Most adults are 60–78 inches in height; few are over 84 inches or under 54 inches. Statistics that fit the bell curve are quite easy to analyse; we can say that 95% of the numbers are within a certain band (two standard deviations in the jargon) and so on.

Hedge fund returns, however, do not seem to be normally distributed. According to Kat, they have fat tails (known in the jargon as kurtosis) – in other words, more extreme events occur than would be expected. They also have a "negative skew": there are more returns on the left-hand side of the curve than should occur.[14] Another problem is autocorrelation, when one month's returns look remarkably like those of the previous month. This may well be because some hedge funds are invested in illiquid instruments. Because they do not trade very often, the prices of these instruments will vary only occasionally. Hedge fund returns thus may move smoothly for much of the time (the autocorrelation) only to jump when a trade actually occurs. This may well be when bad news breaks.

Why should these properties be present? One possibility, which has been mentioned before, is that hedge funds are "short volatility". They are being paid a steady income for insuring the market against extreme outcomes. This means that, for much of the time, they earn a positive amount but then, suddenly, they lose heavily when the extreme events occur. This strategy has been described as "picking up nickels in front of steamrollers".

Neither of these characteristics – negative skew and fat tails – is particularly attractive to investors. At the very least, they make the addition of hedge funds to portfolios as a diversifier more problematic, since the statistical methods for doing so assume a normal distribution of returns.

Alexander Ineichen of the fund-of-funds group Alternative Investment Strategies delivers a robust rebuttal to this academic criticism in his book *Asymmetric Returns*.[15] For a start, he observes that long-only managers are also exposed to fat tails, such as the crash of October 1987. Hedge fund kurtosis arises, he argues, from the small proportion of losing months in the record; when the odd bad month does occur, it makes the numbers look bad. But this is missing the wood for the trees. In the period he studied, all hedge fund losses in down quarters for the S&P 500 summed to 8.5%, while cumulative losses for mutual funds over the same periods totalled 115.6%.

As for negative skew, the single observation of August 1998, when

LTCM collapsed, overwhelms the hedge fund numbers. In fact, as is well known, on average hedge funds have few down months. As for autocorrelation, Ineichen says this is a good thing if one positive return is followed by another. That suggests the returns are not random and that some skill is being used.

So are hedge funds worth the cost? Defenders of the industry such as Simon Ruddick of Albourne Partners say that hedge fund fees are high because they are offering alpha (skill) and not just beta (market return). The fees charged by traditional managers may look lower but a lot of the returns they provide are effectively beta, which can be bought cheaply. Pro rata, clients are paying a lot more for the skill of traditional managers than they are for hedge funds. However, Ruddick adds:

With fees, there should always be an assumption of guilt over innocence. The default position should be that it's not worth it.

Academic studies come thick and fast but they seem to agree on one conclusion: hedge funds do produce alpha. The question is how much of that alpha is kept by the managers. The Ibbotson and Chen study[16] found that hedge fund returns beat the market by around 6.7 percentage points before fees; they took more than half that margin but still left a chunky reward for investors in the form of 3 percentage points of alpha. The paper by Fung, Naik, David Hsieh and Tarun Ramadorai (referred to in Chapter 3) found, however, that, over the past decade, alpha after fees was delivered only by the average fund-of-funds during the short period October 1998–March 2000.[17]

Picking the right fund manager is also difficult; Chris Mansi of Watson Wyatt estimated that only 5–10% of hedge fund managers are skilled enough to add value after fees.[18] Another study by Ravi Jagannathan, Alexey Malakhov and Dmitry Novikov in 2006 found that hedge fund outperformance was persistent, although it tended to decline over time.[19] In other words, past performance was a good guide to future performance. However, David Smith of GAM said in a June 2006 paper:[20]

Past performance is no longer an accurate guide to future risk/ return profiles at either the strategy or individual manager level.

What about hedge funds as a diversifier? A study by Merrill Lynch found that most hedge fund strategies had become steadily more correlated with the s&p 500 index (the main measure of the American stockmarket) over the years since 1997. However, it is not difficult to devise a defence of hedge funds on the correlation point. Certainly, investors would not want hedge funds to be correlated with the stockmarket when it is falling. But why not when it is rising? If hedge funds can take advantage of bull markets and avoid bear markets, surely they are doing their job?

6 The future of hedge funds

Hedge funds are not so much an industry, or an asset class, as a structure. At the risk of being pretentious, you could almost say that hedge funds are a state of mind. This makes them remarkably flexible. So while I said in the Introduction that hedge funds might not even be a separate sector in ten years' time, I will also argue that they will be much more important a decade from now.

How do you square that circle? Hedge funds are moving into more and more areas of finance, using their skills and flexibility to act as banks, insurers and private equity investors. Small funds that started off as two men with an idea and a computer model are becoming diversified giants, with billions under management and offices all over the world.

Perhaps the classic example of this convergence trend is the American hedge fund firm DE Shaw. When it started, DE Shaw used computer models to spot attractive opportunities in equities as a market neutral fund. It has since expanded into several different strategies, moved into long-only management, bought the toy store FAO Schwarz, set up a corporate lending subsidiary, acquired an insurance group, considered a shift into private equity and sold 20% of itself to Lehman Brothers, a Wall Street investment bank. It is no longer just a hedge fund but a financial services conglomerate.

There are four potential types of business dancing round each other: hedge funds, investment banks, traditional fund management companies and private equity groups. Hedge funds could be (and indeed, already are) linked with each of the other three.

Private equity is a topical example. Some companies, such as Fortress, offer both private equity and hedge funds; others, like Cerberus, seemed to have gradually shifted from the hedge fund to the private equity world. Superficially, the most obvious link is their compensation structure: they both generally charge 2% annually and 20% of performance. But perhaps the more profound link stems from the hedge funds' never-ending desire to find sources of excess returns. As financial markets become ever more efficient, one obvious source of excess return is the illiquidity premium: the excess return investors should demand for holding an asset they cannot easily sell. Private equity managers have been taking advantage of this premium for years, so hedge funds naturally want to exploit the same opportunities.

What seems to be happening is an odd combination of competition and co-operation. Hedge fund managers may want to compete by buying stakes in unquoted companies, but they are also ending up as key financiers for the private equity industry by buying the debt used to finance leveraged buy-outs (LBOS).

A similarly odd relationship (part symbiotic, part adversarial) exists between investment banks and hedge funds. The hedge fund manager's most important relationship is with his prime broker, which provides short-term financing and handles most of the fund's transactions. The main prime brokers are investment banks. But hedge funds may also depend on investment bank analysts to generate ideas; those ideas are an important source of bank commission income. Investment banks may also provide hedge funds with custody and administration services, provide start-up advice and seed capital or even invest directly through their funds-of-funds operations.

But a bank that is nurturing a hedge fund may also be competing with it. The bank's proprietary trading desk (which many regard as an in-house equivalent of a hedge fund) is trying to make money in the same markets as hedge funds. Callum McCarthy, the FSA chairman, said in December 2006:[1]

> I find it difficult, if not impossible, to identify an activity carried out by a hedge fund manager which is not also carried out by the proprietary trading desk within a large bank, insurance company or broker dealer.

To some extent this will be a zero sum game; someone must lose as well as win. Indeed, bank trading desks are perceived to have played a large part in driving Long-Term Capital Management to destruction.

Furthermore, bank traders can easily be lured away to join hedge funds by the appeal of a shared performance fee (or indeed, they may leave to start their own fund). If things go well, they can earn far more than the annual bonus the bank would pay them. And when banks have fund management arms, they may be competing against hedge funds to attract clients.

So, if you can't beat them, join them. One way that investment banks and hedge funds will converge is via acquisition. This process really started in 2004 when JP Morgan took a majority stake in Highbridge Capital, a multi-strategy manager. That was followed by a flurry of activity in late 2006 and early 2007: Merrill Lynch took stakes in DiMaio Ahmad Capital, a credit funds manager, GSO Capital Partners, a leveraged finance manager, and Sterling Stamos, a multi-strategy group; Morgan Stanley bought FrontPoint, a multi-strategy manager, and stakes in Avenue Capital, a distressed debt investor, and Lansdowne Partners, which runs both long-short and macro funds; and Citigroup bought Old Lane, a multi-strategy fund run by two former Morgan Stanley executives.

Such purchases can be as much about buying people as buying assets under management. Citigroup installed Old Lane's Vikram Pandit as head of its alternative investment division (and subsequently promoted him, after problems in the group's fixed income division), and Gil Caffray of FrontPoint became vice-chairman of Morgan Stanley Investment Management.

There is nearly always a herd mentality about these trends. If all his competitors are buying hedge funds, it is natural for an investment bank chief executive to consider doing so himself. After all, he would not want to seem behind the times when questioned by analysts or shareholders. In a similar fashion, in the late 1990s every business had to have a dotcom strategy.

Jes Staley, head of JP Morgan's asset management business, was the man behind the Highbridge deal. At the time, there was a lot of scepticism about the deal, both internal and external; the fear was that the hedge fund's real assets, the managers and traders, would quickly disappear. Staley says:

> The premise that drove us into Highbridge was that Wall Street had learned to manage its own balance sheet with sophisticated risk controls. The next task was to apply the same skills on behalf of clients.

Staley also felt that his major competitors were steering clear of the hedge fund industry. "Going in the opposite direction was one way of establishing us as a leading asset management firm," he recalls.

Staley says his success has been twofold: initially convincing the Highbridge management he could keep the bank off their backs and then living up to his side of the bargain. He says:

> The people interested in Highbridge doing the right thing are
> the hedge fund investors. They should be the governors of what
> Highbridge does, not the bank.

The deal does seem to have worked well, with Highbridge soaring from $7 billion of assets at the time of purchase to $34 billion in March 2007 (although its quant fund had a wobble in August of that year). JP Morgan has been able to steer a significant number of its private banking clients in Highbridge's direction.

There are, however, potential conflicts of interest. If an investment bank or big fund management group owns a hedge fund manager, it may find itself going short of the stock of clients (either advisory clients on the banking side or pension fund clients on the fund management side). Since companies do not like those who short their stock, this could lead to angry exchanges and potentially the loss of contracts. This might particularly be the case for a hedge fund involved in merger arbitrage, for example.

There can also be problems when hedge funds link up with traditional fund management groups. Hedge fund managers are usually much better paid than long-only managers; this can cause some resentment. But the traditional groups will have to move into this area. For a start, they need to keep their clients from drifting elsewhere. They have also had to set up hedge funds to prevent their more talented managers from moving to Greenwich or Mayfair.

Another reason hedge funds will meld into the traditional fund management world is that the hedge fund guys have been winning the philosophical argument. It has become more widely accepted that it makes little sense to constrain investment managers if you believe they have the ability to outperform, and hedge funds are the most unconstrained managers around.

Omar Kodmani of Permal says the future of fund management will not be about hedge fund versus long-only but active versus passive. In other words, do you believe a manager has skill? If you do, it is worth paying him fees, and the level of fees may depend on the level of skill. If you do not believe in skill, or you are not convinced that you can identify that skill in advance, you should opt for a passive, index-tracking approach.

The convergence process still has a long way to go. According to Simon Ruddick of Albourne Partners, of the leading 97 hedge funds, around 80% are independent groups and only 10% are part of traditional fund management outfits. Nor will the process be without its hiccups. In May 2007, UBS abandoned its attempt to turn its proprietary-trading desk into a hedge fund. The Swiss bank had set up Dillon Read Capital Management (DRCM) just two years earlier, hoping to entice clients to give money to its fixed income traders. Even though its first fund raised $1.2 billion from investors, that was not really sufficient, given the size of the operation and UBS's hopes. The sluggish start was followed by losses in the early months of 2007, thanks to a bad bet in the sub-prime mortgage market (borrowers with poor credit risks). DRCM was absorbed back into the UBS business, at the cost of a $300m restructuring charge.

Consolidation

As the industry grows, it is becoming more concentrated, perhaps because institutional investors are attracted to established names that have a track record and an infrastructure. According to David Smith of GAM, which keeps its own statistics on the industry, the assets of the 100 largest hedge funds rose to 71% of the industry total in 2006, compared with just 49% in 2002. A number of fund groups have emerged with $20 billion–30 billion under management; the likes of JP Morgan and Man Group have considerably more. The top 100 funds, according to GAM, controlled some $1 trillion of assets.

As noted in Chapter 5, there is some evidence that larger funds can produce better returns, something that is not always the case in the investment industry. There will also be operating returns of scale. If you are running a computer-driven strategy, like the AHL fund cited at the start of the book, you will need back-up power and a disaster recovery site in case of something like September 11th. That is not cheap.

Why not?
Should we do it?

The Ibbotson study[2] did find that size mattered when it came to hedge fund returns. The top 5% of hedge funds by size, with average assets of around $1 billion, achieved annualised returns of 14.4% over the period January 1995–April 2006. The smallest 50% of funds achieved average returns of just 6.8%. This shows that hedge fund clients are being smart; they are generally giving money to the best performing managers.

But not all the evidence points the same way. As noted in Chapter 3, William Fung and Narayan Naik of London Business School found that capital inflows did cause a problem. They found that around 28% of managers showed persistent outperformance. But for those with above average capital flows, the figure fell to 22%. Some believe that small fund management groups are hungrier and earn better returns; as they grow, they become more cautious and seek to hang on to their gains.

The consolidation of the industry is certainly giving the bigger fund managers more power. Lock-up periods (the length of time that an investor has to commit money when a fund is launched) have increased. Investors may also have to give 3–6 months' notice of withdrawals. And gates, which restrict the amount of money that can be withdrawn from a fund at any one point, are now being widely used.

Raising money is also a less happy-go-lucky process than it used to be, when investors were happy to give money to start-ups with a plausible story and a good background in trading or long-only investing. Too many of those start-ups faded away, often because running a hedge fund turned out to be a lot more difficult than it seems.

Nowadays, investors will be impressed only if the manager has been involved with a hedge fund before, as either the number two or number three to some established investor. One seasoned observer of the industry says:

> In the old days, if you had experience and a good track record, you could raise $100m–200m whereas without a track record you could raise $10m–30m. Nowadays, with no track record, you will probably raise zero, but if you do have a track record, you can easily raise $500m–1 billion.

Patric de Gentile-Williams of PCE Investors agrees.

A hedge fund launch used to be a two-man band in a basement
with a spreadsheet and a telephone. Now it's normally the big
guys launching yet another fund.

Gentile-Williams says smaller managers have been caught in a pincer movement. On one flank, increased scrutiny by regulators has raised the cost of running a fund. At a Merrill Lynch hedge fund conference in March 2007, it was suggested that the minimum amount needed to launch a fund had trebled, thanks to legal and compliance costs, over the previous three years.

The attack from the other flank has come from the increasingly institutional nature of the investor base. "Their allocation process is very formal and focuses on corporate structure and risk management," says Williams. A survey by Greenwich Associates in 2006 found that endowments and pension funds had overtaken high net worth individuals as the largest investors in hedge funds.

PCE's business is to offer a platform to smaller managers so they can run money without developing their own infrastructure. "The manager doesn't have to worry about back office, compliance and all the rest," Williams says. It is rather like a hotel or restaurant franchise operation where the company with the brand name provides the basics and it is then up to the individual manager to make the business a success. As of March 2007, PCE ran a stable of 16 hedge funds with assets under management of $900m.

The institutionalisation of the investor base has also changed the way many hedge funds operate. There is much less temptation for a fund to try to shoot the lights out, lest the managers shoot themselves in the foot instead. The industry has changed from the heady days of the 1980s and 1990s, when double-digit annual returns were common. Steven Drobny of Drobny Global Advisors says:

The industry is less incentivised to take big risks. Institutions are
looking for 7–9% returns, so supply goes to where the demand is.

This may not suit the rich people who used to be the backers of the industry. "Historically, hedge fund investors were wealthy clients who would check their statements annually," says Drobny. As a result, they were less worried about short-term volatility. But institutions are used to seeing steady quarterly returns. They also have the fiduciary duty of looking after other people's money; they do not like to be shocked. The move into hedge funds may only have been taken after an argument with some trustees or beneficiaries; one disaster could ruin the whole process.

But hedge funds may gradually be becoming better understood and more accepted by society. Business schools are reporting that graduates are getting excited about joining the sector; indeed, one hedge fund found that its session at Harvard required an overflow room, such was the demand. Gayle Wilson, who is a member of the human resources team at CQS, says it was difficult to attract young and inexperienced staff a few years ago, when hedge funds were generally perceived as risky. The group now runs a summer internship programme for eager hopefuls. Some may fancy themselves as the next George Soros, but more doubtless recognise that the hedge fund sector is one of the fastest-growing industries around.

Hedge funds are competing hard to attract the brightest minds in the academic world. Renaissance's reliance on people with PhDs has already been mentioned. In June 2007, the Man Group announced a near £14m ($28m) investment in the Oxford-Man Institute of Quantitative Finance. David Harding, a former Man employee, has set up academies in Oxford and Hammersmith, west London. BNP Paribas, which part owns Fauchier Partners, has already funded the hedge fund centre at London Business School, and Swiss-based International Asset Management, a fund-of-funds, has supported research at the London School of Economics.

Hedge funds are also recognising that their wealth and power give them a responsibility to the rest of society. In the United States, the Robin Hood foundation channels funds to disadvantaged children, particularly in New York. In the UK, the ARK foundation combines the charitable efforts of many in the hedge fund community. And individual hedge fund managers do their bit, such as Chris Hohn of TCI, who devotes 0.5% of funds under management to a charitable foundation run by his wife.

130-30 funds

As the long-only managers move into the hedge fund world, they are starting to produce strategies that are a kind of halfway house between the two – hedge funds lite. The most prominent to date have been the 130-30 funds. The name refers to the long-short proportions of the fund: the manager can invest 130% of the fund in long positions, and offset this with 30% short. This leaves the fund still exposed to market movements, but clearly the results depend heavily on the manager's skill in stock-picking. The gross positions of the fund are 160% of the assets invested, so some borrowing is involved. If the manager gets the stock picks wrong, or indeed does no better than average, then borrowing costs will mean the fund underperforms the market.

Merrill Lynch reckons that, as of early 2007, pension funds had been responsible for much of the $50 billion invested in 130-30 funds. This makes a degree of sense. Going directly into hedge funds is a big step; the 130-30 fund allows clients to get used to the idea of managers taking short positions (or, indeed, using borrowed money). The early managers in this field have been index specialists such as State Street or big investment banks such as Goldman Sachs.

The idea is that managers have more scope to express themselves within the 130-30 format. In part, this is because of the composition of the indices, which tend to be dominated by a few big stocks and then have lots of constituents that make up a small proportion of the market. Say the manager really dislikes a whole bunch of stocks, each of which has only a 0.1% weight in the index. In the long-only world, the most the manager can do is not own them at all; in other words, have a zero weighting. But this will make hardly any difference to the performance of the fund relative to the benchmark. Allow the manager to go short and those bets can have real value. In other words, removing the long-only constraint should be an advantage if the manager has genuine skill.

But there are still questions about the format. Why 130-30 and not 120-20 or 175-75? Clearly, the figure is a compromise. If the manager were to use more leverage (175-75 would imply gross positions of 250%), investors might be more nervous. However, lower leverage might mean there was little scope to exploit the manager's short-selling skills.

Mike O'Brien of Barclays Global Investors (BGI) says there is nothing particularly magic about the 130-30 format. BGI also runs funds on a 120-20 and a 150-50 basis. But he adds that the information ratio (a measure of the relationship between skill and reward) improves most rapidly as the short exposure rises from zero to 40%.

Some may be sceptical that long-only managers will be able to adapt to the disciplines of short-selling (see Introduction); and fees will inevitably be higher than those on traditional long-only funds (although lower than those on hedge funds). Chris Mansi of Watson Wyatt takes the view that "130-30 funds are artificially over-engineered marketing products". Todd Ruppert, chief executive of T Rowe Price Global Investment Services, warned:[3]

> I think there's going to be a lot of blood on the tracks with 130-30
> products. The view that 130-30 funds will generate a better
> information ratio presupposes that you have the skill to do it.
> Most long-only managers don't outperform the market and that
> is where their expertise is. Now you are going to let them short?

Pyramis, a consultancy, has estimated that 63% of corporate defined benefit pension plans are using or considering funds in 130-30 type formats. It seems likely that the quantitative managers, such as BGI, State Street or AXA Rosenberg, will be best placed to take advantage. Their models should help identify the best short positions. O'Brien says that quant managers tend to be dispassionate about their underweights and overweights, have better sell disciplines and are better at risk control than fundamental managers. However, the August 2007 sell-off showed that 130-30 funds suffered in the same circumstances as other quant-driven strategies.

Permanent capital

It is not just a matter of long-only managers trying to look like or acquire hedge fund managers. Hedge fund managers are moving the other way. Some have acquired "permanent capital", money that investors cannot take away. Permanent capital gives some much-needed stability in a sector where one bad year can cause the business to disappear.

Permanent capital can be acquired in two ways. The first is to float the fund management company itself. The Man Group has long had a stockmarket quote but that is a bit of an anomaly; it started as a commodities broker, and then moved into hedge funds. The prime example in recent years has been Fortress Group, whose initially highly successful flotation showed that investors would attach high valuations to hedge fund managers, even though such managers are reliant on the potentially volatile stream of performance fees.

The second route is for hedge funds to float specific funds on the stock exchange. Once these funds are listed, investors cannot take money away from the managers; they have to find another investor to buy their stake. This idea is as old as the investment trust, introduced in Britain in 1868. Investment trusts have had their own periods of wild popularity (their reputation in America was spoiled by the crash of 1929) but they have one problem for investors: they do not always trade at asset value. Depending on supply and demand, the shares can trade at a discount (which shareholders may agitate to be closed) or a premium (which means investors are paying over the odds).

Nevertheless, this model has a lot of attractions, according to Robin Bowie of Dexion Capital, who runs the largest quoted hedge fund vehicle (Dexion Absolute, a fund-of-funds with a market value of around £630m as of May 2007) on the London market. He says:

> The fund managers get locked-up capital, important for them in
> a world where trading liquid securities to find alpha has become
> more difficult.

In other words, because they know the funding is secure, the hedge fund managers can take positions in illiquid securities where they may feel the potential for profit is higher. Meanwhile, Bowie says, "Investors get what they want, which is a hedge fund with mark-to-market liquidity."

Furthermore, a listed fund may be the most tax-efficient way for a small investor to get access to the hedge fund sector. For UK investors, returns from offshore hedge funds are subject to income tax, not the potentially much lower rates of capital gains tax (CGT). Gains on a listed fund will be subject to the CGT rules.

Not everyone thinks the move to permanent capital is a good idea. Geoffrey Perdon, head of alternative investments at Arjent, says:[4]

> *The permanent capital structure unfairly penalises investors, is undemocratic and demotivates the fund management team to perform.*

This is because the traditional hedge fund structure allows investors to withdraw their money if the manager is not performing well; but in a permanent capital fund investors must find someone else to buy their holding. This may occur at a discount to asset value, causing the investors to take a double hit. Perdon says:

> *We believe that the threat of redemptions keeps a fund manager accountable and this motivation is absent from permanent capital funds.*

Stanley Fink of Man Group is also worried about the discount but for a slightly different reason:

> *A hedge fund itself might be a low volatility fund. But then its assets may be in dollars, but it may have a sterling quote, so you are adding currency volatility on top. And then there will be the discount volatility on top of that.*

The result will be that the volatility experienced by the investor may be too high relative to the return.

Events at Queen's Walk Investment, a listed fund run by Cheyne Capital, neatly illustrate Fink's point. The Queen's Walk fund was exposed to American sub-prime mortgages, the same asset class that caused problems for a whole swathe of hedge funds when American home-buyers failed to service their loans. By July 2007, the trust was trading at a 35% discount to asset value. That is not the kind of "absolute return" investors were looking for. A smaller discount also caused a problem at the Dexion Trading fund, where Financial Risk Management was replaced as manager by Permal in 2007 after disappointing returns.

The market turmoil of summer 2007 seemed to bring at least a temporary halt to the permanent capital bandwagon. The sector's reputation was also dented by events at Absolute Capital, a London-listed manager. The shares plunged first when a star manager quit abruptly and again when it transpired that the funds owned a lot of unlisted (and thus hard to value) American stocks. Investors received a sharp reminder about the lack of transparency in the hedge fund world.

Fees

An obvious problem for the industry, if it is going to take fewer risks, is the level of fees. A 2% annual charge may not seem too bad if the client is earning 15–20%; it seems a lot more when returns are in single digits. So in a world of low nominal returns, you would have thought that hedge fund fees would come under pressure. At the very least, you would have thought that a hurdle rate (the return from cash is an obvious possibility) should be applied before the managers start to earn 20% of all profits.

But so far that does not seem to be happening. The biggest funds-of-funds groups, which have some market power, may be able to get annual fees down to 1 or 1.5% on the funds they buy. Most investors do not have that option; managers will simply turn their money away rather than set a precedent that other clients might follow.

Instead of cutting their fees, unsuccessful managers tend simply to go out of business. And those that have shown a consistent ability to outperform can charge more – 3 and 30 rather than 2 and 20. Hugh Willis, chief executive of Blue Bay Asset Management, says:[5]

> *Demand for well-managed hedge funds exceeds supply of the same by a very wide margin. People are prepared to pay for alpha.*

There may well be a snob value about hedge fund fees. If investors are looking for skill, they are willing to pay top dollar, just as you would not expect to pay $20 for Manolo Blahnik shoes.

The sector that ought to come under most pressure, you would think, is funds-of-funds; after all, they are challenged by clones (see below) and by the ability of large investors to go it alone. But a 2007 survey by PerTrac Financial Solutions, an American data firm, found that the average fund-of-funds fee had stayed roughly unchanged since 2000, at 1.29%; and performance fees had inched up since the turn of the decade.

Some think hedge fund fees should not matter that much, given the benefits managers can bring. Alexander Ineichen of AIS says that "searching for bargains when selecting an active risk manager is somewhat akin to searching for the cheapest parachute". And Drobny reckons: "If we have another bear market like 2000–02, a lot of questions about hedge fund fees will disappear."

But the fee system will always have its critics. In March 2007 investment guru Warren Buffett said:

> It's a lopsided system whereby 2% principal is paid each year to the manager even if he accomplishes nothing, or for that matter, loses you a bundle, and, additionally, 20% of your profit is paid to him if he succeeds, even if that success is due simply to a rising tide.

Cloning

Many investors share Buffett's suspicions. They do not want to pay high fees only to find the manager's skills are non-existent. So academics have tried to break down the returns of hedge funds to discover where they come from. Fung and Naik devised a seven-factor model to explain returns: the S&P 500 index; the differential between small caps and large caps; the return from ten-year bonds; the spread (excess interest rate) on corporate bonds; and three things called "look back straddles", which are essentially trend-following strategies in bonds, currencies and commodities. Since 2005, they have added an eighth factor, the emerging markets index.

The concept of cloning flows from this observation. All the above returns are generated from highly liquid markets, where the costs of trading are low. If we know the factors that are driving hedge fund returns, we can replicate them at much lower cost. After all, these factors are beta not alpha. It is rather like having a robot that can reproduce the exact golf shots made by Tiger Woods.

Indeed, Fung and Naik show that such a portfolio would have returned an annualised 11.6% over the period April 2003–October 2006, ahead of the 10% achieved by the average fund-of-funds over the same period.

Sceptics object that it is always possible to produce good returns by back-testing. Torture the data enough and you will find a formula that works. Usually, however, the formula breaks down when real money is invested in real time. This may be a little unfair since Fung and Naik have been using the same factors since the mid-1990s. They applied the results to the 2003–06 period only because of the emergence of two cloned products on the market, from Goldman Sachs[6] and Merrill Lynch, which used that time series to prove the worth of their models.

However, this approach could still be seen as flawed. Remember that beta represents market risk. So the only portfolio that would have no style or sector bias would be one that represented the entire market. Any portfolio that deviates from the market will have some bias (for example, more oil stocks than normal) and its success or failure will be down to this factor.

Surely there must be some skill involved in selecting those factors. But hedge fund managers do not seem to be getting any credit for it. It is as if a customer had dinner at a Gordon Ramsay restaurant and said: "Yes, this was terribly tasty. But chemical analysis shows it is 65% chicken, 20% aubergine, 10% tomato, 4% flour and 1% paprika. I could have bought those ingredients for £1.50. Why did you charge £20 for the dish?" The chef's reply, if printable, would be along the lines of: "It's all in the mixing."

Nevertheless, the idea that hedge fund returns can be ascribed to a wide range of betas has caused many to speculate whether investors can earn returns similar to those achieved by the industry without paying the fees.

There are two possible problems with this idea. The first is that multi-factor models do not capture all hedge fund returns. Indeed, they might well capture all the betas and none of the alphas. That would be missing the point of investing in hedge funds at all. Harry Kat reckons a rival approach should be used.[7] He says that investors value hedge funds for their unusual properties such as lack of volatility or correlation with other assets. So he argues that you can devise a portfolio with those historical characteristics, made up of widely traded securities such as Treasury bonds. That way, the investor can get the diversification he wants, although he cannot guarantee the returns that will come out.

Another potential objection is that because of the lag in receiving data on hedge fund portfolios, the clones will be investing where the smart money has been, not where it is going. The danger is that the clones will prove too leaden-footed to keep up with the hedge funds and will simply act as the dumb money, only buying what the hedge funds want to sell.

Fung and Naik would say that while individual hedge funds may switch their portfolios around swiftly, the industry as a whole makes only slow shifts in asset allocation. In any case, you could always re-engineer their model so that the clones acted in a contrarian fashion, overweighting the factors where hedge funds are currently underweight and vice versa. You could imagine a whole range of clones, taking slight variants of the hedge fund's position.

The Fung/Naik approach is not the only possibility. Clones could be produced of individual strategies. Some strategies can almost be reduced to a single sentence. Merger arbitrage could be described as "buy the prey, short the predator" and convertible arbitrage as "buy the bond, short the shares". So you could set up a fund to mechanically follow such rules. It would not benefit from a hedge fund manager's skill and judgment on which deals to back, but perhaps their judgment is not worth the fees.

Merrill Lynch has set up one such replicating fund, its equity volatility arbitrage index. This is based on the difference between implied and realised volatility on the stockmarket. Volatility is the scale of fluctuations of a market: whether it rises and falls 1% in a month or 10%. Realised volatility measures how much the market actually moves. When an investor buys an option, the price depends on how much the asset is expected to move; the more volatile it is, the more likely the option will be exercised and the more the option will cost. You can calculate the implied volatility of this option and there is even an index (the Vix) that allows investors to speculate on it.

For complicated reasons, implied volatility is normally higher than realised volatility; the exceptions occur during periods of market turmoil. So a strategy of buying implied and selling realised makes money on average. Merrill Lynch found it returned an annual 14% over 18 years, with only three negative quarters. Whether it will work so well when actual money is invested remains to be seen.

Whether or not they are a commercial success, hedge fund clones seem to be a welcome addition to the investment landscape. As has already been explained, hedge fund indices are often unsatisfactory – indeed, fund-of-funds managers find them easy to beat. Mansi says that "replicators will create a good benchmark". Even some fund-of-funds managers welcome the competition. Smith says: "Clones are a fantastic addition to the market. They should spur us on."

However, Smith adds that GAM attempted to create something similar earlier this decade, hiring some of America's top maths professors to crunch the numbers:

> What we found is that it works for a short term, then it falls apart. The factor analysis suddenly starts failing. The factors don't gradually decline in importance; they go from 40% to zero. Clones will be fine in a trending market but will struggle when the trends break.

There certainly will be some barriers to the acceptance of clones. One oddity is that the investment banks have been among the first to develop such strategies, even though they earn hundreds of millions from the existing industry. Will it make sense, in the long run, for them to compete with their clients?

Future strategies

It is the nature of hedge funds that they are always looking out for new ways of making money. So, just as the industry ceased to be dominated by global macro funds, new strategies will emerge that will change the structure of the industry.

Fink believes that hedge funds can even help save the planet. As a company, Man has taken action in the face of global warming, helping to establish the charity Global Cool, for example, and making the business carbon-neutral. But Fink, Man's deputy chairman, also sees an excellent investment opportunity. When he started looking at the market for trading carbon permits (which create a subsidy for "clean" energy producers by giving them the right to sell credits to "dirty" producers), he noticed that the price varied enormously. "I've never seen a market with such incredible arbitrage opportunities," he recalls.

Man has already gone into partnership with a fund in China that pumps methane out of coal mines and uses it to produce power for the local community. This is a "triple whammy": methane is one of the biggest killers of the miners; it is a far more powerful contributor to global warming than carbon dioxide; and the fund can make money, first by selling the power and then by selling the carbon permit. Fink believes returns could easily be 20% a year, and the fund raised $382m – pretty good for a new idea.

As governments take more action to combat climate warming, carbon markets are likely to become more widespread. Hedge funds, with their expertise and their willingness to provide liquidity to markets, could help get this industry established. Hot money, cool result.

Growth

There was already talk of a hedge fund bubble when the industry's assets reached $700 billion. But that did not stop the flow of funds into the industry, with Hedge Fund Research estimating the total level of assets at $1.7 trillion as of the end of June 2007, with 9,767 funds in operation. Indeed, the first quarter of 2007 saw a record $60 billion flow into the industry. A report by Grail Partners forecast assets could reach $2.5 trillion by 2010.[8]

Hedge funds cannot really be a bubble in the same way as dotcom stocks were in the late 1990s. As money flows into the industry, there is no "price" that rises; hedge funds are investing in a wide range of assets and are often taking contrary positions.

But there is a question of capacity. Although there might be opportunities for a limited number of managers to find alpha, it seems unlikely that 10,000 managers can do so. As some sectors get crowded, hedge fund managers may be forced to pursue ever-tinier niches. Nathaniel Orr-Depner of Lionhart says:

> We have seen a lot more players getting involved. Traders are trying to get between the wall and the wallpaper.

The arbitrage sectors have already suffered a capacity problem when the convertible sector seemed to be overwhelmed by money in 2004 and 2005. But the sector quickly bounced back when the weak players withdrew. It is hard to see how capacity will ever be a problem for long-short equity funds or for global macro. Kodmani says:

*Capacity at a very high level is overblown as a concern, but it is
a concern for some strategies.*

As the summer of 2007 showed, there will always be individual hedge
fund managers that can go bust. Darwinism takes its toll. The industry itself
will inevitably suffer if financial assets of all kinds take a hit (the 2000–02
bear market was largely confined to shares and corporate bonds).

But the idea of going short as well as long, and of aiming for absolute
returns, is now widely accepted as a strategy. The cleverest money
managers will want to operate without the constraints they suffered in the
past. Hedge fund techniques are here for good, even if the industry itself
changes out of all recognition – and 2007's bad publicity will probably
slow its growth.

References

Introduction

1 To be fair, some of this income comes from gains made by investing directly in their own funds. They are eating their own cooking.
2 Reported in *New York* magazine, April 2007.
3 Bernstein, P., *Capital Ideas Evolving*, John Wiley & Sons, May 2007.
4 There are problems with these indices, which are explained in Chapter 5.
5 Reported in the *Financial Times*, July 2007.

1   Hedge fund taxonomy

1 Other people would carve up the industry in different ways. The fund-of-funds group Fauchier Partners divides the sector into two: relative value or arbitrage; and absolute value or directional.
2 It is impossible to do justice, in this guide, to the LTCM saga. Those who would like to know the full story should read either *Inventing Money* by Nicholas Dunbar (John Wiley, 1999) or *When Genius Failed* by Roger Lowenstein (Random House, 2001).
3 Drobny, S., *Inside the House of Money*, John Wiley, 2006.
4 Barclay Group study quoted in *Financial News*, February 26th 2007.
5 Quoted in Bernstein, P., *Capital Ideas Evolving*, John Wiley & Sons, 2007.
6 Efficient market theory states that all available information about an asset is reflected in its price. Thus the only thing that will move prices is news, which by definition cannot be known in advance. Attempting to beat the market by using information (particularly past price movements) should fail. Thus, if efficient market theory was correct, managed futures investing should not work.
7 Speaking at the GAIM conference in Monaco, June 2007.
8 ibid.
9 Brav, A., Jiang, W., Partnoy, F. and Thomas, R., *Hedge Fund Activism, Corporate Governance and Firm Performance*, October 2006.

3 Funds-of-funds

1 Stulz, R.M., "Hedge Funds: Past, Present and Future", *Journal of Economic Perspectives*, Spring 2007.
2 *Asset Size Impact on Fund of Hedge Funds Performance*, April 2007.
3 Kat, H. and Lu, S., *An Excursion into the Statistical Properties of Hedge Fund Returns*, Alternative Investment Research Centre, Cass Business School, 2002.
4 Fung, W., Hsieh, D., Naik, N. and Ramadorai, T., *Hedge Funds: Performance, Risk and Capital Formation*, July 2006.
5 Speaking at the GAIM conference in Monaco, June 2007.
6 Quoted in *Hedge Fund Journal*, June 2007.
7 Speaking at the GAIM conference in Monaco, June 2007.

4 Hedge fund regulation

1 Consultation report, *The Regulatory Environment for Hedge Funds: A Survey and Comparison*, March 2006.
2 Speech to European Money and Finance Forum, December 2006.
3 "Crimes and misdemeanours – and how to avoid each when investing in hedge funds", *Hedge Funds Review*, October 2006.
4 Securities and Exchange Commission, *Implications of the Growth of Hedge Funds: Staff Report*, September 2003.
5 *Funds of Alternative Investment Funds (FAIFs)*, Consultation Paper 07/6.
6 Update of the Financial Stability Forum report on highly leveraged institutions.

5 Hedge funds: for and against

1 Hutton, W., *The State We're In*, Vintage, 1996.
2 Bernstein, P., *Capital Ideas*, John Wiley & Sons, 1992.
3 Brav *et al.*, op. cit.
4 Speech by Callum McCarthy, European Money and Finance Forum, December 2006.
5 As quoted in Connor, G. and Woo, M., *An Introduction to Hedge Funds*, London School of Economics, 2003.
6 Update of the Financial Stability Forum report, op. cit.
7 The point is that banks' liabilities are mostly in the form of deposits,

which customers can withdraw at any time, but their assets are in the form of loans, which can be difficult to realise. So if there is a run on the bank, not only will depositors not be able to get their money back (terrible for confidence) but also many businesses will be forced to close as the banks demand immediate repayment.

8   Khandani, A.E. and Lo, A.W., "What Happened to the Quants in August 2007?", paper available from http://ssrn.com/abstract=1015987

9   Federal Reserve Bank of New York, "Measuring Risk in the Hedge Fund Sector", *Current Issues in Economics and Finance*, Vol. 13, No. 3, March–April 2007.

10 Quoted in *Barron's* weekly, 30th April 2007.

11 Ibbotson, R. and Chen, P., *The ABCs of Hedge Funds: Alphas, Betas and Costs*, Yale ICF Working Paper No. 06–10, September 2006.

12 Kat, H. and Amin, G., *Welcome to the Dark Side: Hedge Fund Attrition and Survivorship Bias over the period 1994–2001*, available at http://ssrn.com/abstract=293828

13 Kat, H., *Ten Things That Investors Should Know about Hedge Funds*, Cass Business School, City University, January 2003.

14 Fat tails can also be known as black swans, an idea made popular in Nassim Taleb's book *The Black Swan: The Impact of the Highly Improbable*, Allen Lane, 2007.

15 Ineichen, A., *Asymmetric Returns*, John Wiley & Sons, 2007.

16 op. cit.

17 This approach can be criticised on the grounds that the academics have used funds-of-funds which, as we know, charge another level of fees. Thus it is possible that the underlying managers have alpha but this is obliterated by the extra layer of charges. The academics' response is that funds-of-funds offer better data to analyse; their records are more complete, they go out of business less often and there is less survivorship bias in the numbers. In addition, they point out that an investor who wanted to build a portfolio of hedge funds would incur considerable research and monitoring costs; fund-of-funds fees are a proxy for those costs.

18 Mansi, C., *Capacity in the Hedge Fund Industry*, Watson Wyatt, March 2005.

19 Jagannathan, R., Malakhov, A. and Novikov, D., *Do Hot Hands*

Persist Among Hedge Fund Managers? An Empirical Evaluation, NBER Working Paper No. W12015, February 2006.

20 Smith, D., *What's the Truth? Turnover and Early Stage Investing*, GAM, June 2006.

6 The future of hedge funds

1 Speech to European Money and Finance Forum, December 2006.

2 Ibbotson and Chen, op. cit.

3 Quoted in the *Financial Times* fund management section, July 16th 2007.

4 Writing in the *Hedge Fund Journal*, May 2007.

5 Speaking at the Fund Forum in Monaco, July 2007.

6 The first hedge fund clone to be launched was the Absolute Return Tracker index, or ART, unveiled by Goldman Sachs in December 2006. Fees were a long way below typical hedge fund levels, at 1% a year; back-tested it would have generated net returns of 11–12% a year.

7 Kat, H. and Palaro, H., *Tell Me What You Want, What You Really Really Want: An Exercise in Tailor Made Synthetic Fund Creation*, Cass Business School paper, October 2006.

8 *Adapt or Die Trying: Darwinism and Intelligent Design in the Hedge Fund Industry*, November 2005.

Glossary

Cross-references are in SMALL CAPS.

Active management
An investment style that attempts to beat the average by choosing between different assets.

Activist fund
A fund that buys a stake in a company and tries to get it to change policy and/or management.

AIMA (Alternative Investment Management Association)
A club for the industry which conducts lobbying and suggests voluntary codes.

Alpha
The investment return attributable to a manager's skill, as opposed to the general movement of the market. Any measurement of alpha should also allow for the risks being taken.

Alternative assets
General term for financial products that are not straight bonds, shares or currencies. Used to describe property, commodities, private equity and, of course, hedge funds.

Alternative beta
Return from position-taking in unconventional markets such as VOLATILITY, commodities or even weather. See also BETA.

Annual fee

The proportion of the fund taken each year by the manager, regardless of performance. This usually ranges between 1.5% and 2% but can go higher.

Arbitrage

A strategy that attempts to exploit areas of the market where assets are wrongly priced relative to each other. Investors will buy the undervalued asset and go short the overvalued one (see SHORT-SELLING).

Autocorrelation

The tendency for one month's hedge fund returns to look remarkably like the next.

Backwardation

A property of the commodities markets, where futures prices are below spot, or current prices.

Bear market

A market where prices are generally falling.

Beta

The investment return attributable to the movement of a market. This can be bought cheaply, via vehicles such as INDEX-TRACKER funds.

Black box

A computer model used by a manager to produce returns.

Bull market

A market where prices are generally rising.

Buy side

The investment part of the financial services industry, including pension funds and hedge funds.

Call option

A contract giving the buyer the right to buy an asset at a given price within a given time period.

Closed fund

A fund that is not open to new investors. Managers usually close funds so they do not dilute returns by being too big for their markets. Sometimes closed funds will allow existing investors to put in more money (a condition known as "soft closed").

Collateralised Debt Obligation (CDO)

A security that bundles together a number of bonds or loans and then slices them up into tranches, based on their risk.

Commodity trading advisers (CTAs)

Quantitative funds that use chart patterns to try to ride on the back of market trends. Despite the name, they do not invest solely in commodities but in a whole range of assets. Also known as managed futures funds.

Contango

When, in the commodities markets, futures prices are above spot prices.

Contract for difference

An asset that gives investors a geared play on a stock. Similar to buying the stock on margin.

Convertible arbitrage

A strategy that aims to take advantage of mispricing in the convertible bonds sector. Convertible bonds pay interest but can be switched into shares (of the same company) under certain conditions.

Correlation	The extent to which one asset moves in the same direction as another. Hedge funds are often described as uncorrelated assets.
Credit derivative	An instrument that allows an investor to insure against (or speculate on) the possibility of a company failing to repay its debts.
Crossing the wall	A term used when an investor is given advance information about a company. The manager should not deal in that security after this point.
Delta hedging	A technique for hedging a position which depends on the sensitivity of the hedge (such as an option) to the value of the underlying asset.
Derivatives	Instruments that derive their value from that of another asset. Examples are futures, options or swaps. They can be used to insure (hedge) a portfolio and also to speculate.
Distressed debt	Bonds of companies that are in trouble. Such bonds will usually trade at a fraction of their face value. Distressed debt managers will seek to buy bonds that are underpriced and will attempt to use their muscle to get value from the bankruptcy process.

Drawdown	A term used to describe a peak-to-trough loss suffered by hedge fund investors. Managers will often use statistics showing the maximum monthly or yearly drawdown of the fund.
Emerging markets	The financial markets of developing countries, such as China, Egypt and Mexico.
Equity risk premium	The excess return (over bonds) payable to shareholders to compensate them for the greater risks involved.
FAIFs (Funds of Alternative Investment Funds)	British designation for retail funds that can invest in hedge funds.
Fat tails	The tendency for returns to be more extreme than a normal (bell curve) distribution would suggest. This makes hedge funds harder to analyse using conventional statistics. Also known as kurtosis.
Financial Services Authority (FSA)	Regulator for the UK financial services industry.
Fixed income arbitrage	A strategy that aims to exploit inefficiencies in the bond markets.

Fund-of-funds   A fund that invests (for a fee) in other hedge funds. As a result, investors get a diversified portfolio. They also benefit from the intermediary's judgment in choosing the best-performing managers and avoiding those with dubious credentials.

Gating   A process used by hedge fund managers to control redemptions during difficult markets. Investors may be limited as to the proportion of their holdings they can withdraw in a given period.

Global macro   See MACRO FUNDS.

High water mark   A figure used in conjunction with the performance fee. The idea is to prevent clients from paying a fee twice on the same gain. Once the fund's value slips below the high water mark, it must rise above it before performance fees start accruing again.

Index-tracker   A fund that attempts to mimic the behaviour of a benchmark, such as the FTSE 100 index or the S&P 500. This can be achieved by buying all the shares in the index, or by buying those that most closely move in line with the benchmark.

Information ratio

A measure of risk or skill. It looks at the manager's excess return against a benchmark (such as a stockmarket index) and compares it with the consistency with which the manager has tracked the benchmark. The higher the ratio, the better.

IOSCO

Short for International Organisation of Securities Commissions.

Kurtosis

See FAT TAILS.

Leverage

The use of borrowed money to enhance returns. A fund that is three times levered has borrowed three times as much as investors' capital. When the hedge fund manager gets things wrong, leverage can severely damage returns.

Lock-up period

The period for which an investor commits not to withdraw his or her money. This ranges from weeks to years. These periods allow the fund manager to undertake complex strategies in illiquid instruments (and using borrowed money) without having to worry about the need to meet REDEMPTIONS.

Long-only

The way that money has traditionally been managed. Investors buy assets they believe will rise in price.

Long-short

A strategy that combines long positions with short (see SHORT-SELLING). The resulting portfolio gives some protection against market falls and takes advantage of the manager's stock-picking skills. This is one of the most popular hedge fund strategies because it is the closest to long-only; both managers and investors feel comfortable with it.

Macro funds

Funds that take big positions in share, bond or currency markets based on their views of how economic trends will develop.

Managed account

A separate account run on behalf of a hedge fund manager for a single investor. It gives the investor the benefit of transparency.

Managed futures funds

See COMMODITY TRADING ADVISERS.

Market neutral funds

Funds that try to eliminate stockmarket risk. They consist of equal long and short positions. Provided the manager picks the right stocks, the fund will rise in value, regardless of the market's direction.

Merger arbitrage

A hedge fund strategy that speculates on the result of takeovers.

Multi-strategy fund	A fund that gives money to a range of in-house managers in a range of fields such as CONVERTIBLE ARBITRAGE or DISTRESSED DEBT. The man-in-charge switches money between sub-managers on the basis of his judgment. An alternative to FUNDS-OF-FUNDS.
Mutual fund	A traditional investment vehicle, usually owned by private investors. In Britain, they are also known as unit trusts or OEICS (open-ended investment companies). As in a hedge fund, investors can only buy and sell their holdings from the fund management company.
Net asset value (NAV)	The total value of the portfolio, after debts have been deducted.
Over-the-counter	Instruments that are not traded on a financial exchange.
Passive management	An investment style that seeks simply to mimic the performance of a benchmark, at low cost. Also known as INDEX-TRACKING.
Performance fee	A payment that gives the manager a share of the returns in the fund. Usually, this is one-fifth of the fund's returns, after the annual management fee has been deducted. In other words, if the fund makes 25%, the manager takes 5%.

Portable alpha

A tactic that allows an investor to get exposure to a manager's skill in a particular market without being exposed to the movements of the market itself.

Prime broker

An arm of an investment bank which services a hedge fund, providing finance and custody services, lending shares, introducing the manager to potential investors and so on.

Private equity

Investing in companies that are not quoted on a stockmarket. Private equity funds often buy entire quoted companies, using a lot of debt. They cut costs and improve management, and then sell the company back to the market several years later.

Put option

A contract giving the buyer the right to sell an asset at a given price within a given time period.

Quant manager

An investor that uses statistical models, generated on a computer, to identify profitable opportunities.

Redemptions

The act of withdrawing an investor's money from a hedge fund.

Replication

The idea that hedge fund returns can be copied (at lower cost) by buying and selling various combinations of assets.

Securities and Exchange Commission (SEC)

Regulator for the US financial services industry.

Seeding

Early funding of a hedge fund.

Sell side

The broking part of the financial services industry which tries to persuade investors to trade in securities.

Sharpe ratio

A measure that compares returns with the risks taken. The ratio divides the return minus the risk-free rate (usually short-term interest rates) by the STANDARD DEVIATION. The higher the ratio the better.

Short-selling

A strategy that bets on falling prices. The manager borrows the asset (at a cost), sells it in the market and then hopes to buy it back at a lower price.

Side letter

Separate agreements made between a hedge fund manager and individual investors. For example, some investors may get lower fees or shorter redemption periods.

Skewness

In a normal distribution, a bell curve applies with numbers evenly distributed either side of the average. But hedge funds are not always like this. Skewness measures how they differ. Negative skew means there are more down months than you would expect.

Sortino ratio

A variant of the SHARPE RATIO. Since investors do not normally care about VOLATILITY when they are making money, the Sortino ratio looks at only downward volatility when measuring the STANDARD DEVIATION.

Standard deviation

A measure of VOLATILITY. For hedge funds, usually defined as the average difference between each return and the mean return. The more the returns are bunched together, the less volatile the fund is deemed to be.

Statistical arbitrage

Hedge funds that use powerful computers and mathematical formulae, known as algorithms, to try to take advantage of anomalies in the financial markets.

Stop loss

A tactic used to limit loss on a position. The manager arranges in advance to sell a position if it falls by a set amount.

Structured products

Financial products that adapt a pool of assets to appeal to different investors. In the hedge fund world, they have been used to offer investors a guarantee of getting their money back, in nominal terms, after a certain period; this is designed to reassure investors who fear the sector is too risky.

Technical analysis

Using chart patterns of previous price movements to predict future changes in asset prices.

UCITS III

A set of European Union regulations that has given mutual fund managers more flexibility to use hedge fund techniques.

Value-at-risk	A measure of the riskiness of a portfolio, usually relating to the maximum loss in one day's trade.

Volatility	The size of fluctuations of an asset or portfolio. Some hedge funds treat it as a discrete asset class.

APPENDIX
HEDGE FUND FACTS AND FIGURES

A1

Estimated growth of assets
Hedge fund industry 1990–Q3 2007, $

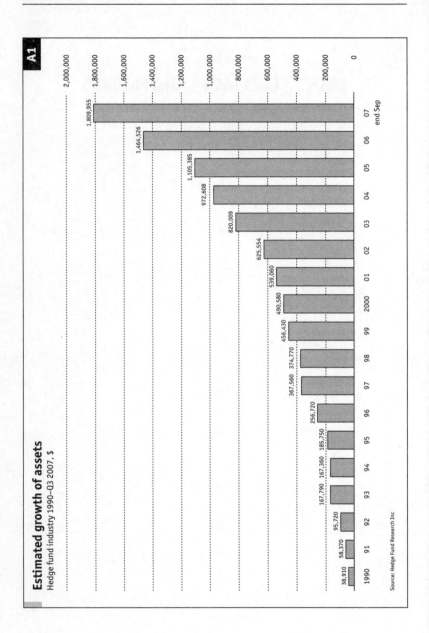

end Sep	
07	1,809,955
06	1,464,526
05	1,105,385
04	972,608
03	820,009
02	625,554
01	539,060
2000	490,580
99	456,430
98	374,770
97	367,560
96	256,720
95	185,750
94	167,360
93	167,790
92	95,720
91	58,370
1990	38,910

Source: Hedge Fund Research Inc

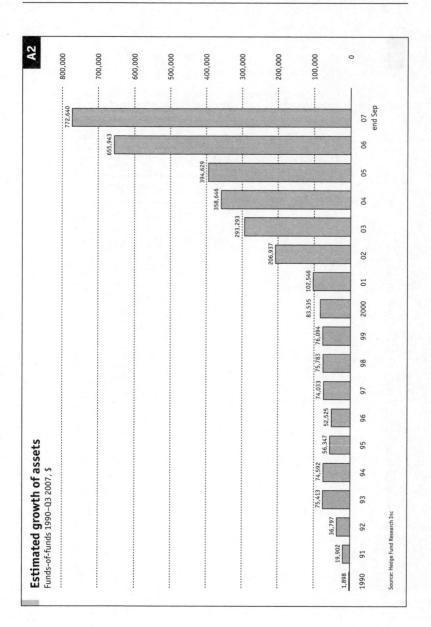

A2

Estimated growth of assets
Funds-of-funds 1990–Q3 2007, $

Year	Value
1990	1,898
91	19,902
92	36,797
93	75,413
94	74,592
95	56,347
96	52,525
97	74,033
98	75,783
99	76,094
2000	83,535
01	102,546
02	206,937
03	293,293
04	358,646
05	394,629
06	655,943
07 end Sep	772,640

Source: Hedge Fund Research Inc

129

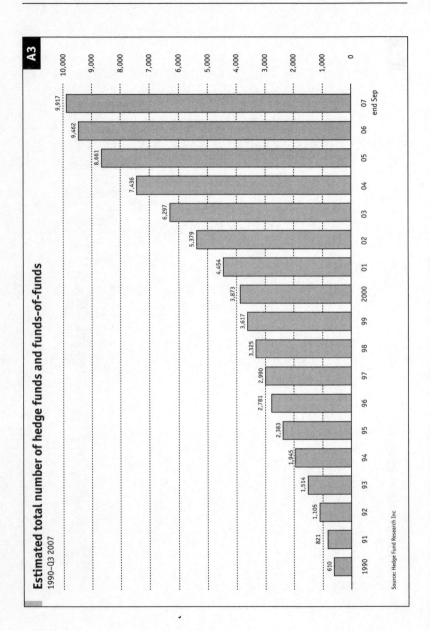

A3

Estimated total number of hedge funds and funds-of-funds
1990–Q3 2007

Year	Value
1990	610
91	821
92	1,105
93	1,514
94	1,945
95	2,383
96	2,781
97	2,990
98	3,325
99	3,617
2000	3,873
01	4,454
02	5,379
03	6,297
04	7,436
05	8,661
06	9,462
07 end Sep	9,917

Source: Hedge Fund Research Inc

130

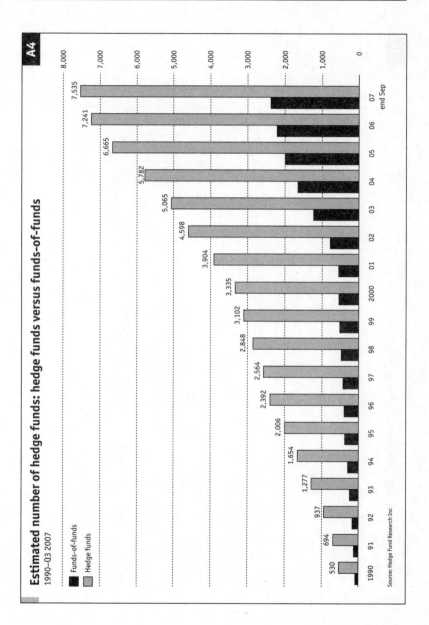

Estimated number of hedge funds: hedge funds versus funds-of-funds
1990–Q3 2007

■ Funds-of-funds
□ Hedge funds

A4

Source: Hedge Fund Research Inc

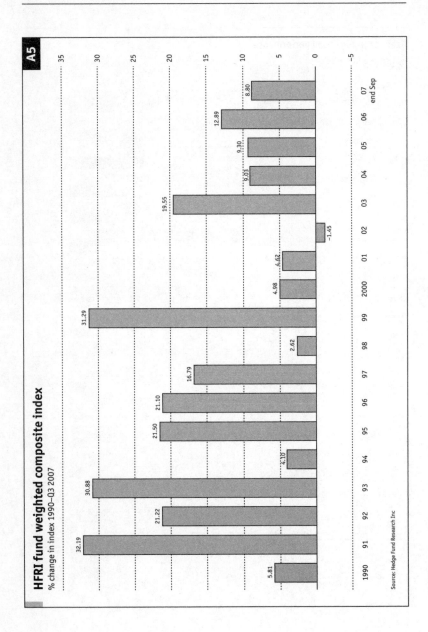

A5

HFRI fund weighted composite index
% change in index 1990–Q3 2007

Year	Value
1990	5.81
91	32.19
92	21.22
93	30.88
94	4.10
95	21.50
96	21.10
97	16.79
98	2.62
99	31.29
2000	4.98
01	4.62
02	-1.45
03	19.55
04	9.03
05	9.30
06	12.89
07 end Sep	8.80

Source: Hedge Fund Research Inc

Table A1 **Hedge fund performance**
% change in index

Index	2004	2005	2006	2007[a]
Convertible Arbitrage	1.18	−1.86	12.17	4.74
Distressed Securities	18.89	8.27	15.94	5.66
Emerging Markets	18.42	21.04	24.26	20.24
Equity Hedge	7.68	10.60	11.71	9.69
Equity Market Neutral	4.15	6.22	7.32	4.16
Equity Non-Hedge	13.32	9.92	15.95	12.58
Event-Driven	15.01	7.29	15.33	7.35
Fixed Income: Arbitrage	5.99	5.60	7.28	2.34
Fixed Income: Convertible Bonds	7.90	2.49	20.78	7.93
Fixed Income: Diversified	6.16	5.21	7.63	1.75
Fixed Income: High Yield	10.49	5.27	10.78	0.01
Fixed Income: Mortgage-Backed	11.86	7.86	8.70	2.03
Macro	4.63	6.79	8.15	7.88
Market Timing	6.42	14.40	16.84	7.08
Merger Arbitrage	4.08	6.25	14.24	6.96
Relative Value Arbitrage	5.58	6.02	12.37	6.58
Sector (Total)	11.34	9.14	16.31	10.02
Short Selling	−3.83	7.28	−2.65	0.52
Fund of Funds Composite	6.86	7.49	10.39	8.08
Lehman Bros Gov't/Credit Agg Bond	4.54	2.55	4.07	4.30
S&P 500 w/ dividends	10.87	4.91	15.78	9.13

a To September.

INDEX

Page numbers in *italics* refer to
Figures.